REFLECTIONS ON PRIVATE PRAYER

REFLECTIONS
ON
PRIVATE PRAYER

Mike Endicott

Christian Publications International

First published in Great Britain by
Christian Publications International ("CPI")
an imprint of Inspiration – Assurance Publications
PO Box 212 Saffron Walden CB10 2UU UK

Online references cited in this book are correct at the time of publication.
Online material may be deleted or reassigned at the copyright holder's
discretion. Readers are reminded that such material may be transient in duration.

Cover design by Justyn Hall at J8 Creative
Email: justyn@J8creative.co.uk

www.christian publications-int.com

Readers are encouraged to compare assertions in all CPI
books with the clear witness of Scripture. CPI offers this book
as a contribution towards continuing study of the
inspired Word of God, which the publisher considers to be
the final 'court of appeal' in matters of faith and doctrine.

ISBN 978-1-913741-05-1

Printed in Great Britain by Imprint Digital, Exeter
and worldwide by Ingram Spark

Contents

As always, I ask the reader to compare everything I say or write with what is written in the Bible and, if at any point a conflict is found, always to rely upon the clear teaching of scripture.

Mike Endicott

PROLOGUE

'The true treasure of the Church is the Most Holy Gospel
of the glory and the grace of God.'
*Martin Luther (1483-1546), Luther's Ninety-five Theses,
Harold J. Grimm, ed., Fortress Press, 1957, thesis #62, p. 14*

'Oh, no!', I hear the cry, 'Is this another dreary missive on prayer?'

No, this is something very different. Of all the various forms and styles of prayer that exist throughout the world, here we focus only on our need to find a way of effective private prayer, for personal solution preferences, and this book directly addresses our doubts on the subject. This little book does not set out to teach a method of praying that will 'get' God to do what we want; how to pray, or when to pray, or what to pray for. It does try to recognise, importantly, that the great movers and shakers of this world quite simply are not who we might think they are – our celebrities or politicians or economists, our armies or our diplomats. The real change-makers in the world are those who pray.

How can this be? Readers may believe they already know how to pray, but they may not. They may be comfortable with their prayer life and they may be disappointed with it. They may enjoy a full and devout life of prayer and they may only send up infrequent 'rocket' prayers when troubling circumstances demand.

Most of us will be living somewhere in the middle, between the extremes. Whether it is good or not so good, effective or of little help, we can step together through these pages and, by the grace of God, find ourselves in a newly vibrant and rewarding world of prayer. Can we do that?

A man at home one day came across a nail in a piece of wood which seemed to be in the wrong place, not doing anything useful but generally getting in the way. He determined to pull it out. Full of confidence that he knew perfectly well how to extract unwanted nails from pieces of wood, he grabbed it with a pair of pliers. It would not move. Then he grabbed some larger and stronger pincers, only to arrive at the same result. Next, he wired the handles of the pincers together and introduced a lever between them. He slipped a fulcrum under the lever so that he could get a number of his friends to exercise a greater purchase and more pulling power. They all sweated and heaved and managed to shift it only a little. He had thought long and hard over the problem, had built and tried increasingly complicated methods of 'doing it' and, like many a prayer life, found only disappointment. He had not realised that it was not a nail but a screw. Had he just known to twist and turn it, it would have come out easily.

Two tools of extraction, pliers and screwdrivers, are hugely different. The simple idea that we might be in need of a different prayer tool, and a completely different way of unscrewing messy things, is so challenging, so radical, so new, so commonly undreamed of that, if anyone suggests it to many spiritual people they might easily shrug it off and dismiss the idea.

We prayer-givers have a variety of styles and methods for trying to draw the nail from the wood, both in our own circumstances and in those around us. But allow me to suggest a screwdriver! It is radically different from the pair of prayer pliers that usually comes easily to hand. We are all called to be agents of change, and here, in the issuing of the right and appropriate tools for the job, lies a set of far more hopeful and trustworthy answers.

The aim here is to rediscover, to swing open afresh, what might be a new gateway to the reader – one already unlatched, freed for access, when the curtain in the temple was torn from top to bottom, tearing open forever the boundaries between heaven and earth for all to see.

It is here, through the all-powerful, loving kindness of Christ, that heaven is revealed and spills into the world. Where heaven and earth overlap – where living in the kingdom on earth proves it impossible to tell the difference between those two – lies the kingdom of God. That kingdom of God is very near and the pleasure of God is to work with us in prayer partnership to thicken the kingdom's influence and to widen its reach to save every one of his children from the mess we struggle through, living as so many of us do, out and beyond the refreshing and restoring shade of its divine influences.

I had supposed since childhood that prayer was a private thing unless led publicly in some church meeting. It is an 'up and down' kind of thing, sometimes successful and often generating only silence from above. Like most people I have met, I have been unwilling to talk about it with anyone else in case they thought I might be doing the wrong thing, saying the wrong words, pushing God around for lack of faith, not assuming anything would necessarily come of it. Yet it always seemed a good idea at the time.

Even so, rather than dismiss the subject as a frivolous waste of time, the need to discover more crept gently and slowly up on me. The teaching and the promises of Jesus during his human earthly ministry could not possibly be a mere gust of hot air!

The day when the dawn of any new understanding of the subject was only a faint glow on my horizon, I looked for direction. A new journey needs a new map to hand and it arrived, funnily enough, on the forecourt of a new car showroom. After weeks of exploration, my wife and I had at last seen a model which suited our needs very well. The salesman was enthusiastically extolling the virtues of all the safety features built into the latest models. There was no end to the lights that flashed when things might not be quite right and more bleeps than could be heard in our kitchen on a heavy cooking day! There were cameras all around that viewed and displayed every potential hazard, and there were bags all around that would explode on contact with any foreign body, to give protection in any unforeseen incident.

At that very moment the most extraordinary and illogical thought came into my head, and it was this: all these wonderful devices would surely help protect us once we had met with such an accidental time, but they would all be quite pointless without a steering wheel! Of course it did have one installed, but imagine what it would be like without it! All the safety devices in the world would be of little use compared with the basic installation of a steering mechanism. There were plenty of gadgets to warn of the results of impending loss of control, but all drivers need to start by steering straight down the road! A way of steering, in the first place, is fundamental.

'Is prayer your steering wheel or your spare tyre?' asked Corrie ten Boom (1892-1983), see *Clippings from My Notebook*, (Nashville: T. Nelson, 1982), p. 64.

What, I prayed, could be my wheel, my fundamental way of steering any new walk in the kingdom? I started with Christ's teachings to disciples.

> Then they asked him, "What must we do to do the works God requires?"
>
> Jesus answered, "The work of God is this: to believe in the one he has sent" (*John 6:28f.*, NIV).

In this context, believing in someone means two things; that we trust them and that we are willing to do what they ask us to do. Confidence and obedience are both involved in believing in someone.

The twelve apostles had been asked, straightforwardly, to go forth, teaching the good news of the kingdom of God and healing the sick. Then, Jesus had instructed us to pray like this: '... your kingdom come, your will be done on earth as it is in heaven....' It seemed apparent from this that Jesus wanted us to see the planet we live on to be, through prayer, just like heaven in the sense that his wishes should be carried out equally in both places. That way, heaven and earth would be inseparable. Living in this world would be like living in heaven. The kingdom of God is heaven on earth.

Re-examining the Scriptures led to a simpler, more solid appreciation of God's expectations of the very early church and, as a consequence, a need to understand his kingdom a little more and his desire that we proclaim it. After all, how could we possibly do what Jesus wanted the church to do if we did not have a good working knowledge of the kingdom?

So it was that, face to face with those in physical and emotional suffering, armed with this freshly gained knowledge of the kingdom of God, and with the scripturally derived gifts of Calvary's cross, we began to approach the sick and the injured by announcing to them the good news that the kingdom of God is near, and the benefits of the cross of Christ. Instead of asking God to turn up and do something for anyone in trouble, we learned to worship, to offer prayers that are thank-offerings to the throne room above. That approach to extending the kingdom – praise and thanksgiving rather than pleading prayer – really did put the horse back in front of the cart.

I have since gone on to discover that praying the same way in private is not actually praying in private at all. It is a team effort. What is more, everyone is picked for a trial with the team. All of us. No one chooses to play for the club – the Manager chooses us. We have all been picked! As with any activity that needs us to be fit, to learn the team rules and to follow team strategies and tactics, we need to practise. Without putting in the time and the effort, we may well be good enough to keep a temporarily selected place on the village team, now and again, but there is much more on offer with 'Team Kingdom'. Seeing much 'greater things than these' is the promise of God.

The problem with private prayer, for me, has been this: it has, in the past, been such an unreliable source of help as to be almost not worth the bother. Armed with my Bible as my steering wheel, I set off to seek the kingdom and the role of change-maker we are called to play in it.

The first thing I fell into was a world of great joy. This kind of joy is not a self-satisfied and gushy grin, neither is it a matter of being naturally and permanently jolly. Joy comes simply from living in the knowledge and the flow of God's desires in growing harmony, because our souls delight themselves in God himself.... Living in this stream of ever-flowing grace, through private prayer, leads us to rejoice in God's desires and in nothing else.

I hope that these pages will help anyone of us bow down our heads and hearts before God and allow his kingdom desires, the divine desires of God, to be done.

'Be joyful always' (1 Thessalonians 5:16).

FOREWORD

By the late Revd Dr Winfield Casey Jones, US pastor and deep friend of the author.

This week I read a quote from a favourite theologian, Karl Barth. He said: 'To clasp the hands in prayer is the beginning of an uprising against the disorder of the world.'

I would like to unpack what he said, and to refer to some words of Jesus which I think are behind what Dr Barth wrote. Let me begin with two questions about that quote. First of all, why would he say there is disorder in the world? And secondly, if there is disorder, mustn't it be God's will?

Why say there is disorder in the world? God created a perfect and orderly world, but because of human sin and because (as a result) we live in a fallen creation, the world God created is clearly no longer the world we live in.

We live in a world where children die, where wars kill, where famine rages, and where some people are still literally enslaved while others live in bondage to fear, hatred and addiction. In so many other ways the fallenness of the creation and of our lives is evident. Without a doubt, we live in a broken and fallen world.

Second question: Are all these evil things that happen in the world God's will? Of course not! Why else would Jesus have taught us to pray like this:

'Father...your name be hallowed, your kingdom come, and your will be done on earth as it is in heaven.'

Clearly, Jesus knew that there is a great gap between Earth and heaven. On Earth, God the Father's name is not yet honoured, his kingdom has not yet come, and his will is not yet done. But isn't God sovereign? Couldn't he destroy evil in a heartbeat?

As a patient at a cancer hospital I have noticed that cancer doctors have a problem: They want to kill cancer without killing the patient. Even though he is God, the Lord faces a similar problem—he could destroy sin and evil in a moment, by destroying us, the host. But he desires to destroy the disease of sin while saving us. Apparently this is a process.

God's Son, Jesus, began the process of salvation long ago in his atoning death and in his resurrection victory over sin and death. That same Jesus tells us to pray for the full implementation of that victory—for earth to become like heaven. He knew that praying for the coming of his Father's kingdom is very important. Such prayer is an act of revolt against the sinfulness and fallenness of our world. Such prayer is also an act of loyalty to the Creator/Saviour God and to his eternal kingdom which is breaking into our world, in which we now live by faith, and which eventually will be the only reality there is.

Pastor Casey

PART ONE

Private Prayer: the Dynamic Framework

Chapter 1

SO LET'S GO SKIING

My readers know that I love to talk about the kingdom of God by using analogies. These stories are sometimes called 'parables', but that is a bit presumptuous in my case. Jesus, being wholly God as well as wholly human, told parables much better than I can. My own analogies cannot be examined too deeply, unlike the parables of our Lord. I do believe that stories may help those who have difficulty grasping the point.

There is a particular and extremely common human failing. We know what we know, and we lock our knowledge of what we know up in a box. When I get the lid of my box shut, I feel secure with what is inside. Try to teach me anything different, something that does not easily slot into my box alongside its existing contents, and I will argue, vigorously defending my position, or failing that I will just ignore what you are saying to me. We all do it.

Jesus' disciples had been listening seriously to his talking about kingdom issues for a long time and were beginning to get it. The secrets of that kingdom were opening up to them.

Unhappily, those with other agendas of their own just could not get to grips with the true kingdom idea. They asked him why he spoke all the time with parable stories.

(Jesus) –

'The secret of the kingdom of God has been given to you. But to those on the outside everything is said in parables so that,

> they may be ever seeing but never perceiving,
> and ever hearing but never understanding;
> otherwise they might turn and be forgiven!'
>
> > (*Mark 4:11–12*, NIV).

It is easy to ignore teaching on divine prayer partnerships when it makes us feel insecure or unworthy of the task. It is easy to pick and choose bits and pieces from it that will fit our own faith as it stands. Jesus was calling for something very radical – calling us to unlearn a great deal and start afresh – but our tendency as human beings is to be ever seeing but never perceiving, and ever hearing but never understanding. If it does not fit the box we subconsciously ignore it in the hope that it will fly away.

My sixteen year-old grandson, Tom, has returned from his third school skiing trip. A week in the mountains with school friends – how exciting for him. When he was a new beginner, they placed him on the nursery slope under an instructor who specialised in teaching young novices. Tom was learning fast but, on the second day of his first trip to the snow, he spied some grown-ups off in the distance, flying down the mountain, off-piste. Oh, the freedom! They were caught up with the spirit of the adventure and were thoroughly enjoying every moment of it. Tom wanted this. He wanted to go off-piste. He wanted the freedom of expression and the adventure of it all. But he was to be very disappointed. His more responsible instructor forbade it, telling him to stay where he was and learn the basics well before trying anything else.

So many of us who pray for others, so many of us whose 'box' contains all sorts of ideas and experiences we learned from other people and from our own trials and observations, long for the off-piste freedoms of working in the Spirit. However, we desperately need to get the theory under our belts before we do too much practice in praying. Tom needed a new affinity with balance, speed and snow, and we need a new affinity, too. We need to spend time on the nursery slopes of prayer, building our prayer partnership with Christ before moving on to working with him in kingdom spreading.

Sitting down heavily on the lid of my box with a great dismissive 'humph!' towards those who teach something a little different than that which I already know, may be just the exercise of my pride. I hope not!

Whenever I have done anything that seemed 'good', it might have been just that – good – but as I seek first the kingdom of God, all the rest begins to happen naturally, to fall off the back of the wagon. Imagine what a powerfully skilled prayer army we would belong to if we all tried going back to the kingdom nursery slopes and starting afresh by developing a working relationship with Our Lord!

What is the first step? How can we start a greater partnership to see 'greater things than these'?

Chapter 2

WAITING IN THE PADDOCK

I spent many months, long and hard ones, looking for a wider and sharper understanding of the business and the benefits of prayer. Casting around the press, radio and television news bulletins, it seems that the world has so much wrong with it and, despite the earnest prayers of many, God sometimes seems so reluctant to dive down here and help us. We prayer-givers send up 'rocket prayers' when we need him but I could never describe those desperate demands as working with God to build the kingdom and improving the abundance of life. I wanted so much more. I wanted to become available to be an agent for change in the world, not only in times of family sadness, sickness, aches and pains but also in major international man-made and natural disasters and their appalling effects, together with anything he was planning, and everything in between.

Jesus has promised us in the Bible that we should be seeing 'greater things than these' but I was seeing little sign of anything greater than his healing deeds. It turned out, quite shockingly, that although I might claim to be on the right lines in ministry I was a long way off-beam on the subject of personal, private prayer. What an experience it has been and still is, turning so many carts around to follow the horse! I wonder, nowadays, if my understanding of the nature of prayer, my cart, was being pulled along only by a group of traditional 'sacred cows' which have had to be unyoked and released before I could swing the cart through a hundred and eighty degrees. Much of that progression has been very hard to come to terms with, but the joy of getting there is immeasurable.

With this dilemma came a fresh thought, that perhaps I should be seeing God even more seriously as being who he is – an agent for change himself. There is a dreadful tendency among we Christ-followers to treat God as an ATM, jumping across the street when short of a blessing, to plug in a prayer card and press the buttons. Jesus taught that we should seek first the kingdom of God and that all the things we need would then be added unto us. As King of God's kingdom he ought to know! That is a complete reversal of rocketing 'ATM when the need arises' prayers. Seeking first the kingdom would mean seeking not some instant gratification but seeking to build a harmonic relationship with Jesus; and should such a thing be possible at all, the riches of heaven would then certainly flow more abundantly as fallout, as a direct result. It is easy to see such a turnaround as if it promises to be a more reliable way of getting God to perform, but it is quite the reverse. It is seeking a deeper harmony with God, whose overarching plans are to bring his whole family home to live with him. If God wants our relationship to be that way, then will it be possible to grow into it? If we can, then what will follow will follow. 'All these things will be added to you.'

The more I checked out the prayers I followed in church, the ones I heard around me and the ones I offered up myself, the more I saw them falling into two distinct categories: kind-hearted rocket praying, directed with not too much expectancy toward a 'maybe, maybe not' God and the type of prayer life I was drifting into. For ease of description we can distinguish these two types from one another by calling them the common 'ATM' prayers and kingdom 'prayer partnerships'. The first of those is self-explanatory and reviving the second is refreshing, exciting and most rewarding.

I have always found the best approach to such apparently upside-down thinking is to sleep on it and, in the very beginning, sleep was my first approach. It was in that uncertain, uncontrolled and hazy world between sleeping and waking one morning that I felt as if the early sun pouring in through the dream-induced cottage bedroom window was warming me into semi-awareness.

Still daydreaming, still living in my dream. I sat up and glanced out of the tiny upstairs window in this little dreaming world to catch sight of the corner of a paddock that appeared to lie alongside my life's 'chocolate box' cottage.

In the paddock were jumps for horses, one or two very big, almost unassailable ones, and plenty of smaller ones that looked low enough to step over, all getting in the way and all ripe for some horse riding practice. Some of these obstacles changed shape as I stared at them, taking on the appearance of some of life's more monstrous difficulties, unassailable, high and troublesome but, I wondered, might I be able to clear them and put these fences behind me, if only I had a horse? It would be worth having a go.

Still dreaming, leaping out of bed, showering and then dressing in all the right riding outfit, getting myself into the right frame of mind and grabbing all the right equipment, I pulled on my riding boots and strode out into the yard toward the outbuildings.

I beat on the stable door and called out the horse's name. Silence. I hammered on the stable door again and again with clenched fists and with the same result. Had the horse gone to sleep? Had he bolted? Was he in there alright but just in a sullen, anti-Mike mood?

Shrugging off my disappointment, I put the horse's absence to the back of my mind and turned back to the house, walking down the side of the paddock, staring angrily at the immovable fences. It soon dawned on me that the only way to get over those fences would be for me to climb over them in my own strength, and to chop, saw, hammer or dismantle them myself. Or do so with a little help from my friends. Failing that, I would just have to live with them.

Then I saw the horse out of the corner of my eye. He was watching me out of his. He had been standing quietly in the paddock all the time, watching me! I called out to him: 'What on earth are you doing here? You should be in the stable where you belong! That's where I put you, that's where I keep you so I know where to find you when I need you.'

'You can beat on the stable door to attract my attention all you like,' he replied, 'But actually this is where I live these days. I am here all the time already. The fences in your paddock are there to be overcome and I'm here to do just that. But I need you to ride with me to do it. That's the way horse riding is supposed to work. You and I do it together. It's a working partnership. You ride with me and I do the jumping. Neither of us will do it alone. On my own I can only stand and gaze at the obstacles and at you walking by. On your own you can only stare with horror at the difficulties in your way and glance hopefully in my direction. So saddle up and climb up and we will get the job done together!'

It seems sometimes that so many of our prayers go unanswered. So many, in fact, that we lose our expectancy of God to a greater extent than we may be prepared to admit. Yet faith, according to the Scriptures, is essential.

If we admit such things as unanswered prayer then we would indeed be speaking the truth, but not the whole truth. There is much more to be said before we can reach any conclusion about such things.

For too much of my Christian life, I have been approaching the subject of prayer from the wrong angle. If the sight of oncoming fences across my life path upset me, then I would go to the stable doors of heaven for help. Sometimes God appeared in answer, but then often he didn't.

It came as a real shock to realise that all answerable, righteous prayer emanates from God in the first place. That is part of the plan. It is because he wants the kingdom to grow to the point where it eventually returns completely to that wonderful and wholesome state we could describe as the 'Eden life' condition. Having put the thought of prayer on a particular subject into our heads he then expects us to work with him, first of all in prayer, to see the desired goodies (heaven's riches) achieved.

Happily, since eventually finding the horse already living in the paddock, I don't go knocking for help on the stable door any more. Not very often, anyway. The best way to pray is to listen, hear and obey his voice and pray accordingly. This is not a spiritual gift given only to the holy, it is achieved, like horse jumping, through practice. This can get easier, It can lead easily to a life of productive prayer that sees his kingdom come, his will being done on earth as it is in heaven.

In seeking first his kingdom I tend to wait until God puts a prayer need into my head and I take it as coming not from my own understanding but from him in the first place – if it is a righteous thought. Then I pray in the full knowledge that we are pulling together, him and me, against the troublesome fence. I put in the prayers and he puts in the power and the skill.

This needs practice. Getting 'good' at anything needs practice.

Chapter 3

THE KINGDOM GLOWS

'What's in this prayer partnership idea for me?' might be a common cry as we glance sideways at the Church. Insiders can often have real difficulty hearing such a cry when, truthfully, we might be making the same call about our own prayer life: 'What's in it for me?'

Actually, we do have a rough idea of an answer. We have taken nearly two thousand years to shape and reshape the subject of prayer the way we want it. Our personal understandings and practices satisfy most of us but fulfil precious few who suppose there must be more to the good influences of God in this messy world. We organise things the way we want them to run. We can work out for ourselves what we want from God and when we want it, but dare we ask what God wants from each of us?

One of the bigger answers to that question is 'partnership', partnership in service of course, but first and foremost, partnership in prayer. Calling God my prayer partner? How could I possibly justify such an outrageous suggestion? So where should I start? Where did this idea of working with God in partnership come from?

The Bible starts with the account of Creation. Then, inside that story, we have a description of life in the Garden of Eden. There have been great debates, for a long time, about the process that Creation must have gone through. There is this scientific theory and that other one, and much discussion on whether or not the latest scientific or the original Biblical versions should be taught as 'historical truth' in our educational systems.

The argument missing from the scientific versus the scriptural debate is that this particular story was written as a picture or a blueprint – the world as God wants it to be. It portrays a life where heaven and earth appear to be the same place, the kingdom of God/heaven. It's God's picture of a perfect world, of Paradise. In it, God created us to be in his own image.

Then God said, 'Let us make mankind in our image, in our likeness, so that they may rule over the fish in the sea and the birds in the sky, over the livestock and all the wild animals, and over all the creatures that move along the ground.'
So God created mankind in his own image,
in the image of God he created them;
male and female he created them.

Genesis 1:26–7, NIV

God saw all that he had made, and it was very good.

Genesis 1:31a, NIV

This Eden garden is described as 'very good'. It should be; it is God's own vision for life, our lives. It is the blueprint for the kingdom of God on earth. It is the most superb place to be. In that divine dream there is no pain, no sickness, no aggression, no disease and no tears. There is no family breakdown; there are no war orphans, no armies, no battles; all is love, joy and peace. That all sounds too good to be true, idyllic beyond all sensible possibilities, but as dreams go, it is real enough.

So here we are, in that story, and here comes Adam, faultless man. He is freshly created by God, unblemished by the results of wrong living and the normal scars of everyday life. He has a number of roles to play, the most important one being that he is a human being built to reflect the character of God. He is showing us what God is like; he is publicly demonstrating God's character. At least, that is how it begins!

This view of the kingdom of God with us today seems a long way from today's popular understanding of its being merely another name for heaven, somewhere we might somehow relocate into, if we are good enough, when we die. The simplest view of the complete truth is that God wants, has always wanted, heaven and earth to be the same place. That is his dream for us.

Adam messed up terribly but all is not lost. God made a second man, Jesus, exactly like himself, initially to do the same job of showing us all what God is really like.

Having filled this first main objective, Jesus was put to death for heresy simply because, they imagined, he did not teach God and his kingdom dream the same way the powers-that-be wanted to teach God themselves. They had gone down the wrong lane and were refusing to turn round to see him for what he truly was: the Son of God. Giving up his life on a cross, Roman style, was a perfect payment for all our wrong-focused tendencies in life, and God the Father in heaven brought him back to life, elevating him to his rightful place at his own right hand.

Ascending back to heaven he did not take the kingdom with him. It is still here and he has left us to grow it in partnership with him and by the grace of his Holy Spirit.

The fact remains; earth is supposed to be like heaven by God's doing but, at the same time, it remains a mess by human doing. Where we (God together with us) succeed in making them the same again is called the kingdom of God. That looks like an impossible task, and yet it isn't. Why not?

Jesus can do anything on his own to mend the 'mess', to

extend the kingdom of God, heaven on earth. He has given the Church an instruction to teach the world what he taught his disciples – that the kingdom of God is near us. To cap it all, he then promises to stay near to us 'until the end of time' (see Matthew 28:18).

This is a perfect picture of a working partnership, where he provides all the power to mend things according to his will, and on our part, through prayer, we open up the world's 'black spots' and ready them to receive his grace. Our part in the partnership is to open trapdoors in our world to accept heaven's mending. This is the divine deal on offer – we make the paths straight for him and he puts in the world-changing love power. We work at it together. To grow such a dynamic working partnership we need to look much further than perhaps we are used to.

Adam and Eve (in a snapshot depicting the ongoing movement of the whole human race to this day) turned their backs (as most of us are quite used to doing) on the life that God wanted for us, and had to leave that perfect paradise in a hurry. This act in darkness, as it were, causes the light to split apart.

This appalling drift is like an iceberg breaking away from the seaward tip of a glacier. Nowadays we are all standing on the iceberg as it sails away from the mainland shore, drifting further and further away on the currents of this worldly life - our world which contains hatred, sadness, unrest, impatience with one another, anger, a general lowering of too many human standards, disloyalty, viciousness and self-seeking. Then add pain, sickness, grief and sorrow to this mess and we know we are all very far from the home that God dreams of. The greatest sadness is that we are actually rejoicing in our freedom to make these bad choices and constantly seek to take down more and more God-based standards of life.

The prophecies in the book of Revelation (Apocalypse)

of St John the Divine reveal that God's purposes will be fulfilled. We can look forward to a new heaven and earth.

This is some of what John wrote:

And I heard a loud voice from the throne saying, 'Look! God's dwelling place is now among the people, and he will dwell with them. They will be his people, and God himself will be with them and be their God. He will wipe every tear from their eyes. There will be no more death or mourning or crying or pain, for the old order of things has passed away.'

He who was seated on the throne said, 'I am making everything new!' Then he said, 'Write this down, for these words are trustworthy and true.'

Revelation 21:3–5

Changing the world we live in, bit by bit, towards that event is what we are looking forward to as we pray, 'Your kingdom come'. The kingdom of God (firstly pictured in the garden of Eden) gradually re-colours and refocuses all our troubles.

Certain things become apparent from all this; firstly that the 'Eden' life was perfect for Adam and Eve (who I see as representing mankind). It was a perfect and abundant blueprint for Creation, with nothing in it that could separate anyone from the love of God.

Secondly, life as we know it today is very far from God's 'Eden' idea. We may indeed enjoy many of its benefits but our lives are also tainted with too many examples of the opposite.

Thirdly, we are excited to know that Jesus is coming back, and our lives will be wholly immersed in his love and goodness.

Fourthly, we can rejoice in recognising God's purpose

because it is apparent that his will is to repair the damage caused by our 'turning away'.

Fifthly, we are to be aware that the kingdom is really already operative here on Earth, as Jesus showed, taught and lived. It will also be manifest more widely, as prophesied in scripture, but we can begin to participate in it now, as we walk in obedience to his call. The kingdom is within us as we live under his kingly rule, and there is more to come, and we acknowledge this when we pray in the prayer Jesus gave us. "Your kingdom come" is about both the present and the future. Of course, we do not know when this kingdom will be completely restored, but what a hopeless life it would be if we had no hope of it and no access to it meanwhile.

We are very much welcomed to join in – in 'kingdom prayer partnerships', to help in the mending. The best place for a prayer-giver to stand is in the stream. The Father sent the Son. Then the Father and the Son sent the Holy Spirit. Then the Father, the Son and the Holy Spirit sent you and me. We who are praying in Christ are being directed in the same God-decided direction. To do what, exactly? To proclaim that the kingdom of God is near – very near and very available.

My difficulty was this: not giving myself up to being carried downstream by the current of God's recovery-plan, (something that began to occur naturally as I set about the business of allowing a prayer partnership with him) had meant I was constantly swimming against the current, and thereby the kingdom around me remained almost stuck in the mud of my comfortable status quo! I have found it possible, privately, to turn around. Anyone can begin to 'go with the flow' by growing into a new and vital prayer partnership with Christ and starting a private life of action – in prayer that sees the world about us change as the light of heaven expands and the kingdom grows around us to the glory of God.

Chapter 4

THE WRONG TURNING

Most of us, our family, our friends, our relatives as well as the family and friends of our friends, one way or another, seem to have something going on in our lives which we would not think of as being 'wholesome' in kingdom terms. Prayer lists for some can become so long, the burden of them becomes too heavy. That leads easily to despair at life itself and a sense of hopelessness inside.

The real problem we all have is that we, the human race, were designed (in God's original Eden plan) to live in the closest contact with him. That is our natural living space. Outside that natural environment, our bodies, minds and spirits, everything that makes us complete human beings, can be badly affected. This alternative atmosphere we have ended up breathing instead is too cold and too thick – full of dangerous ideas that, unknown to us, lead to all the nasty conditions of mankind.

The unpalatable truth is that, looking at it from a spiritual point of view, we grope about our lives in the darkness of our own closed eyelids, our own turning away. Once we have shut out the light of God's Eden-portrayed dream, life gets much more complicated. We get muddled up in our understanding of what light really is. Too many of us have come to believe that darkness is light and light is darkness. Our vision of God is all bundled up into a mess. We have trouble seeing God for who he really is. I wonder, along with many others I am sure, if there was anyone else down through recorded history who has been quite so terribly misunderstood.

In the Bible's account of creation, when Adam and Eve originally turned their backs on God and left Paradise, they turned down the wrong lane and we have gone on travelling that downhill way ever since. We seem to revel in doing this because downhill is easy, tumbling over ourselves, tripping over our own feet and damaging ourselves in the process, going faster and faster and further down the wrong road. We have found that making bad decisions is a great deal easier than making the right ones and we commit that error regularly and continuously. Living in the wrong lane allows us the freedom to 'enjoy' self-centred living to the full.

The road we are on leads to separation, as far away as we can make it from God. The further we go, the darker it gets but, as we teach ourselves that darkness is in fact light, we remain happy while it all goes well. Happily, this separation is something that exists in our minds alone and not in God's. He has stayed with us in the world but, because of our turning away, he lives with us as a stranger, unrecognised.

He is actually slightly nearer to us than he ever used to be, following closely behind us. He is only one step behind. Jesus is God eagerly following us down this slippery slope, saying to us in 2 Chronicles 7:14,

If my people, who are called by my name, will humble themselves and pray and seek my face and turn from their wicked ways, then I will hear from heaven, and I will forgive their sin and will heal their land. (NIV)

His arms are outstretched for us, as always. Stopping, turning around and falling into them is the first step to building a wonderfully new prayer partnership with him. This first step may be the most difficult but it is worth it. The next ones are so rewarding!

Chapter 5

THE KING'S POLICIES

Continually turning back into his arms, looking up and out of myself, I find I am gazing at a staggering thing I had never seen before with such a degree of clarity, and it is this: God has devoted all his 'planning' to installing a programme of creation recovery and restoration right across the whole planet. The plan has already started; it is up and running.

This royal plan is divinely designed to achieve one major aim: to attract and enable all of us to turn back and set off along the road towards home, to draw us into the kingdom of God/heaven, and to live with us again in the holy and wholesome state illustrated in the Bible picture or vision of the Garden of Eden. It is a plan to restore the Eden life to all of us, not when we die but during our lifetime.

Every one of us is called on to join in this particular plan and to do it not just by doing good things for other people worse off than we are, but through this God-given gift of a prayer partnership with Jesus, doing kingdom building together with him.

Any one of us is capable of doing more than merely pray but we cannot achieve much more than pray until after we have prayed. It is here we often seem to trip up rather badly, if we do not fall on our faces altogether. We slip easily into thinking we can do our bit well enough where we are (or where we are going) by doing whatever we plan to do when we get there. Having made up our own minds that what we are about to do is 'a good thing', we pray that God might bring his presence and power into this particular piece of good work. However, praying firstly for his direction, rather than praying for his support after we have made the decision for ourselves, always yields significantly more fruit on the job. That is because the work undertaken is more likely to be in the detailed flow of his purpose for our individual actions.

For reasons anchored somewhere in the great depths of his love, he needs us to take on a supporting role in his world changing plan. We are part of it. He intends to use us as agents for change. We can catch sight of one tiny piece of this vast programme by realising one fundamental aspect of its design – that the route of grace going from God to anyone's heart is through someone else's heart. For that purpose we are all involved, all invited to play a part.

His plan is to work exclusively with us to see this recovery project advance. He openly offers to work alongside us as a prayer partner, in order to progress the plan. Is there a Scripture basis for such a radical idea? Yes indeed – it is all there in Luke 12:32-40,

'Do not be afraid, little flock, for your Father has been pleased to give you the kingdom. Sell your possessions and give to the poor. Provide purses for yourselves that will not wear out, a treasure in heaven that will never fail, where no thief comes near and no moth destroys. For where your treasure is, there will your heart be also.

'Be dressed ready for service and keep your lamps burning, like servants waiting for their master to return from a wedding banquet, so that when he comes and knocks they can immediately open the door for him.

'It will be good for those servants whose master finds them watching when he comes.

'Truly I tell you, he will dress himself to serve, will have them recline at the table and will come and wait on them.'

'It will be good for those servants whose master finds them ready, even if he comes in the middle of the night or toward daybreak.

'But understand this: if the owner of the house had known at what hour the thief was coming, he would not have let his house be broken into.

'You also must be ready because the Son of Man will come at any hour when you do not expect him.' (NIV)

I was thrilled to discover three important points when looking at Jesus' teaching here. Firstly, God's being pleased (or in other translations 'God's delightful decision') to give the kingdom to us is the same description as the divine pleasure being expressed at Jesus' birth (see Luke 2:14) and after his baptism, as well as his overt pleasure in revealing some of the kingdom secrets to children.

Then again, the Greek verb used here to express his pleasure is in the past tense, meaning that this is a past and done action. In other words, God's decision has already taken place. We are not trying to get God to give us anything – that decision has already been made. We seek God's kingdom precisely because God has already decided to give its wonderful life to us.

To repeat the definition, 'kingdom' doesn't simply mean eternal life with Jesus when we die, our post death condition of life. Here 'kingdom' is talking about the same kind of effective influence in heaven which Jesus is now building on earth through his prayer partnerships and ministries with us. It involves his love influencing human hearts, minds, bodies, relationships and actions. I have come across these fields of influence stretching over things personal, interpersonal, State and inter-state, governmental and between governments, the potential disasters of extreme weather events, climate changing and other worldwide conditions. God has delightedly decided to include us in expanding the scope of his loving, reconstructing influence so that who we are and what we do is significantly change for the better, in kingdom terms. Our involvement in the plan makes us agents for change if and when we follow the stream of the dream rather than decide for ourselves what his directions ought possibly to be!

Implementing the major strategic step of his great plan, God himself came down from heaven in the person of Jesus to start it going. Coming as a human, he was clearly demonstrating that the plan needs humans to work with God to further the kingdom's objectives. Working through other human beings is always best. To join in, I needed to know how to get 'into the swing', to pray in a working prayer partnership with him. Would he be able to work with me, with all my shortfalls and failures?

Dorothy Leigh Sayers (1893-1957), wrote this in *Christian Letters to a Post-Christian World*, (Eerdmans, 1969):

For whatever reason God chose to make man as he is –limited and suffering and subject to sorrows and death – He had the honesty and courage to take His own medicine. Whatever game He is playing with His creation, He has kept His own rules and played fair. He can exact nothing from man that He has not exacted from Himself. He has Himself gone through the whole of human experience, from the trivial irritations of family life and the cramping restrictions of hard work and lack of money to the worst horrors of pain and humiliation, defeat, despair, and death. When He was a man, He played the man. He was born in poverty and died in disgrace and thought it was well worthwhile.

So he will include even me! Of all the secular and religious organisations, skills and practices that exist to help us to mend lives, injustices and ungodly situations, the prayer partnership with God is easily the most powerful and effective agency that has ever been put into our hands. To understand this at all to its widest possible extent, we need to define the business of prayer partnerships.

Here I found another horse straining to find its proper place at the front of the cart.

Essentially and surprisingly, the main flow of prayer is the way in which God communicates with us, rather than the way we tend to prefer it – us communicating with him. It is the other way around.

It seems we are to be kingdom Ambassadors, posted 'overseas' (out there in the world). True and righteous prayer always emanates from God as any earthly government's policies and strategies emanate from the Ambassador's own home government. Prayer is not a method of persuading God to do what we want. It does not provoke him into decision-making. It is not an attempt to enlist his help or even to win him round to our way of thinking. Ambassadors do not spend their time in foreign places, calling on the strengths and influences of their own home government, either economic, political or military, when they see things that don't sit easily with them. They know their government's views and policies inside out and project those opinions into those uncomfortable situations they come across in their work.

Whatever the situation is that might prompt us into prayer, the yearning to pray that way originates from God. He takes the initiative in all righteous prayer – these things always start with him. My realising this, that the beginning of every good prayer initiative comes directly from God's heart, has been absolutely foundation-building in my newly rewarding prayer life. It raises within me (it would with anyone) a natural 'water table' of trust, the essential building block of any relationship. It serves to underline the basic necessity of listening to what God wants prayed for before any action takes place. The direction we follow, to be counted as righteous in this context, has to be by his instruction.

This one radical thought, this one 'horse before the cart' idea, such a reversal in my traditional perception of prayer, stays uppermost in my heart as I walk on to find constant renewal in my prayer life. All rightly pious prayer emanates from God. He thinks of it first and then places his thought in our hearts to chat over with him.

That is our God. Prayer does not and cannot change his view of things because each right and good thing we might ask for he has already thought about and put into the plan. What it does do, however, is change God's actions in this one sense; it is our willingness (expressed by our asking) that opens doors, giving him the opportunity to carry out what is already in the plan to rebuild and recover our lives.

We agents for change, we prayer-givers in partnership with God, open a gap in the world to let in the grace-light of heaven. We listen to what he wants to do, pray for it to happen and make straight the way of the Lord. Then he can move. That is the working nature of anyone's prayer partnership with Christ.

Chapter 6

A MASTER CLASS

At this point we need to turn the prayer cart around so that the horse is out in front, leading and directing, doing the pulling. Prayer, I have discovered to my joy, is not overcoming God's possible reluctance but getting involved in his willingness.

I have come to this from a long history of serving in prayer without ever realising that I needed to turn the whole thing around at its very beginning.

Changing my concept of prayer so radically from back to front has not been easy. I had always thought of God as a supplier of goodies, in terms of 'getting' prayers, but have found to my intense joy, that it is so much more rewarding to be an accepted part of his team for kingdom implementation rather than just a passing kingdom pickpocket! Once into a private working partnership in prayer, the world opens to this ministry. On my own I have just been a pickpocket for 'gracelets' but with him – he is changing the world!

This change, putting the horse before the cart, was not easy. I think of it as a steering lock problem. An old friend once offered me a ride home in what, I suspect, was an even older car. We were, at least, pointing in the right direction! We had to drive it up a steep slope onto the road, which then swung away to the right. Then the ride would be downhill most of the way home. The car would not start. My driver friend kept leaning on the ignition key until the battery was almost flat. No joy. Then along came a colleague with, would you believe it, a tow-chain in the back of his truck.

'I'll haul you up to the road,' he offered. 'Then you should take a right, put the car in forward gear and let the speed come up a bit down the hill. Then slip the clutch. That'll bump start her OK!'

I just love optimism. He linked up the chain to the front of the old car and hauled us up the slope, turning right at the top in the hope of going down the hill. We got to the top. The car would not turn right. Something was badly wrong. Panic! We couldn't turn the steering wheel. We were heading straight across the road towards an ugly, deep ditch. Any second now this was going to be nasty.

My old friend, the driver, yanked his right fist down as his knuckles went white, gripping the wheel. Nothing changed. More panic! We went straight on.

Then I could breathe at last. Our colleague hauler had seen the problem in his rear view mirror and stood on his brakes. We stopped. He climbed out of his cab and sauntered back to us along the chain with a straight face and raised eyebrows, nonchalantly reaching in through the driver's open window and, without comment, turned the key, releasing the steering lock, saying nothing, amazed at the shortage of our common sense; then he turned around and sauntered silently back to his truck.

This long ago memory returned to me one morning recently while I was praying to understand better my tiny part in the future of the kingdom this side of Jesus' coming back. My wonderings led me to this thought: here I was seeing a picture of a pair of established prayer-givers being towed along uphill by the traditions of our habits of praying. Unhappily and unaware, our steering lock was firmly in the 'ON' position. We were locked onto our current prayer routes – the pursuit of God, when we wanted and for what we wanted.

We try all sorts of ways of making our prayer experience

more comfortable, more satisfying for us, more attractive to church visiters and strangers alike, but all to little avail because the direction ahead is fixed. It is straight on into the ugly ditch, whatever we try to do.

Of course, Jesus always knew, practised and taught better than this. His kingdom teaching did not even have a steering lock on board. His idea of our fellowship with him was something very different than what we, in our inclination to go our own way, have lurched into down the centuries without even noticing it. He was kingdom partnership orientated. Could it be that we are 'Father Christmas orientated' instead without realising it? What a difference!

All would not be lost if only our religious 'car drivers' would realise, just for one single moment, that something is mis-aligned. We are heading in the right straight line direction but steering is almost impossible! The attractions of social justice programmes and our personal steering locks, our comfortable satisfaction with the status quo, is far too tightly engaged.

To re-position the horse, as it were, I went back to the study of the promises of God, back to the glorious person of Jesus, back to seeking first the kingdom above everything and then proclaiming it at every opportunity.

'Oh, no!' we may cry, looking around the other passengers in the car. 'Will they ever be interested in anything other than the status quo? Won't they always pray tomorrow the same way they did yesterday because it is the only way they know?'

I was so blessed when I got to the top of the slope, the initial learning curve as it were, and realised I needed to make a right turn. I had the angel's prompt to switch off the steering lock and now I am sailing home! It is a narrow switchback road with many sharp bends and cliff edge turns and other cars on the opposing carriageway with full-on headlights, but it is the kingdom road. I am sure it will be a long journey but it is going home!

The fundamental basis of kingdom-stretching prayer is not contained either in our form of words or in the manner in which we address God with them. It is in something else entirely – it lies in having a right relationship with him, a holy working partnership, the horse before the cart. We sit on the cart's driving seat and follow the horse. We learn to listen and follow him. Strangely enough, we are not teamsters. We don't pull the reins this way and that to steer the horse, we hold them lightly in our fingertips, picking up the signals coming back down the length of the reins and, surprisingly, we steer the cart to follow the horse.

Clearly, the only practical basis of relating to God in this way is Jesus. It is only through him. We outlawed ourselves by turning our backs on him. Though we are designed and built to be in touch with God, the human condition is that of having broken away from him and being unable to repair the damage ourselves.

Jesus came. He was both entirely God and entirely man. Nothing has changed in that today we can reach back to our heavenly Father God through Jesus, and only through him.

The blood shed on his cross is the basis of all prayer. It is only through the 'buying back' business of his dying that the sought-after relationship that underlies all our prayer is established . I can come to God through Jesus to get my having ignored him straightened out. Only as I keep in step with Jesus in what drives my prayer life can I seriously practise prayer, staying involved in his kingdom-stretching activities.

Jesus' own words make the plan for this God-designed prayer partnership very clear. We have been left, in the Gospels, two groups of teachings on prayer over the three and a bit years of his teaching ministry. The first group appears about half-way through. The second group comes towards the end, during the evening of the last day. He gave us altogether eight promises over prayer and six of them are here in this group. Matthew 18:19–20, is the first one.

'Again, truly I tell you that if two of you on earth agree about anything they ask for, it will be done for them by my Father in heaven. For where two or three gather in my name, there am I with them.' (NIV)

That is to say, if there are two of us praying, there are three. If there are three meeting up to pray together, there are actually four involved. There is always one more in the room than we can see. It does not follow from this that church prayer groups may not exceed three in number, neither does this teaching imply that Jesus would not be with us were we on our own. In fact, the wonderful thing about private prayer is that he is indeed with us in prayer partnership, on our own, so long as we remain in the flood and flow of the Father's will. One of us might be thinking: 'He won't listen to me: I'm not good enough!' But then we can, all of us, do, think and say things that are not right. Whenever falling into that trap myself, I can quickly fall back on this: the Father always hears Jesus. Wherever rightly motivated hearts are at prayer, Jesus is with them taking their prayer and making it his own prayer.

The second of these passages is Mark 11:22–24.

'Have faith in God,' Jesus answered. 'I tell you the truth, if anyone says to this mountain, "Go, throw yourself into the sea," and does not doubt in his heart but believes that what he says will happen, it will be done for him.

'Therefore I tell you, whatever you ask for in prayer, believe that you have received it, and it will be yours.'

I know this is true as long as I remain in the flow of his kingdom dream for the world. Actually, it is not reported that Jesus moved a physical mountain. I cannot imagine a mountain moving sideways into the sea. I live in Wales, surrounded by mountains and plenty of sea, and yet I can't, for one moment, imagine it happening!

We often want to feel, instinctively, that these statements need some sort of deep and careful explanation: a few boundaries put up around them to keep them within our own experiences.

What are God's own boundaries? The last four of the six are in John's Gospel, talked over on the night he was betrayed. John wrote down much of what was said for us here in John 14:13–14,

> 'And I will do whatever you ask in my name, so that the Son may bring glory to the Father.
>
> 'You may ask me for anything in my name, and I will do it.' (NIV)

It is so encouraging to read him repeating the promise to give it emphasis. Then we have John 15:7,

> 'If you remain in me and my words remain in you, ask whatever you wish, and it will be given you.' (NIV)

That word 'remain', or in other translations 'abide', is a strong word. It does not mean to be a regular church member or even to make some phone calls or to hire a night's hotel room, or to put up a garden shed or a gazebo at the bottom of the garden. It means moving into a close and totally reliable prayer partnership to stay.

There is nothing directly said here about God's will but there is something said about our wills: 'and it will be given

48

you.' Or, a little more literally, 'I will bring it to pass for you.'

The practical meaning of Jesus' words here (in my own translation) is this: If you abide in me and you are steered by my thoughts, then please ask me for what is your real desire to ask for. I will lay myself out to bring that thing to pass for you. That is the force of the words. This same chapter, sixteenth verse:

> 'You did not choose me, but I chose you and appointed you to go and bear fruit—fruit that will last. Then the Father will give you whatever you ask in my name.' (NIV)

God had our prayer partnership with himself very much in mind when choosing us. The last passage is John 16:23, 24,

> 'In that day you will no longer ask me anything. I tell you the truth, my Father will give you whatever you ask in my name.
>
> 'Until now you have not asked for anything in my name. Ask and you will receive, and your joy will be complete.' (NIV)

On the subject of prayer, this group of statements must be the most overarching to be found anywhere in the Scriptures. There aren't any limits on who should pray or what to pray for. However, I have been able to find three limitations imposed: the most effective prayer goes through Jesus; the prayer-giver should seek first his kingdom, to know it and to love it; and the prayer-giver is to have trust.

The partnership relationship that underlies prayer has an all-absorbing purpose. That governing purpose is to please Jesus – not ourselves but him. Real prayer is not so much an act but an attitude – an attitude of dependency, dependency on God. It is living closely with him so that there can be common lines of thought between his mind and ours. It is the vehicle God has appointed to communicate the blessings of his grace and goodness to his people. To make this a reality we need him to fill our minds with his thoughts and then his desires become our desires, flowing back to him in our prayers.

We pray: 'Your kingdom come. Your will be done.' The kingdom of God does not come because we try to squeeze God's will into our own lives. It has only come when your will is completely aligned with his will. That is the developing prayer partnership with God.

Chapter 7

THROUGH JESUS

We prayer-givers have to work at attaining harmony with God. Without that, our prayers may simply be pumping air. I have found it so easy to fall into the 'goodness trap' of thinking that because God is good then anything I want to pray for that seems to me to be good must be a right thing to pray for. Seeking the kingdom of God and harmony in prayer partnership within it are different. It is being a member of an enormous team, waiting for the Captain to direct the flow of play, and then, hearing the commands, doing what he wants us to do. We have to get in line with the constant flow of divine thinking about the people, the planet, the universe.

Any divine partnership of prayer works through Jesus. The prayer itself must be offered in his name because the entire strength of our prayer partnership lies in him. Let us bear in mind that we have no standing at all with God except through him.

Let us imagine we know an extremely wise and clever judge who knows a great deal about family law in some overseas country, not our own. Imagine he goes over there to try a case before their courts in which he has been having a great deal of particular interest. He is intrigued. His sense of justice is firing on all cylinders.

It would not work. Why not? I'm sure they would politely ask him to leave! He would not have any legal standing in that country. His presence and his enthusiasm to steer things according to his own sense of what is right would simply not fit the bill overseas, however good at his job he might be.

Now, it is the same for us. We human beings down here have no standing at the bar in heaven's courts. We are, in effect, disbarred through our natural inclination, as a species, to turn away from God. We can only come to that court through someone who has that kind of recognised standing. Only through him can we come.

When we do come in Jesus' name, it is as though Jesus himself is praying. In my own prayer life it is as though Jesus tucks his arm through mine and takes me up to the Father and says something on these lines: Father, here's a friend of mine; we get on well together. Please give him what he asks for, for My sake.

This imaginary conversation only works for me because I have devoted my prayer life in latter years to harmony first, seeking first the kingdom of God and his righteousness and his righteous purposes. I find in the same conversation that the Father quickly stoops and graciously says to me something along these lines: What will you have? You can have anything you ask for when my Son asks for it.

God the Father is predictably responding to the knowledge that Jesus the Son and I would not be together in front of him unless my request was absolutely in line with Jesus' thinking and that, consequently, it would be absolutely in line with his own wishes. Of course that is all in the sense of how I feel at the time, but that is the practical effect of our asking in Jesus' name – when, and only when, we know what we are saying.

I would encourage everyone to practise devoting themselves primarily to growing the harmony of their prayer partnership with Jesus, before anyone is left to cast doubt on the deep truths of praying in the kingdom.

Through Jesus Christ Our Lord.... To use his name like this was never meant to be the trundled-out ritual ending to a prayer request. It is too deep for that. Those words imply that we are praying in total harmony with God's thinking on whatever is the issue at hand. That thought heavily emphasises our need to get to know him much better. His name must never be a throw-away phrase in ending a prayer.

Using Jesus' name directly adds a very sharp spearpoint to what we do. In the final analysis, the force of using Jesus' name comes from the fact that he is indeed the victor over evil. Prayer is repeating the Victor's name into Satan's ears and insisting on the latter's retreat. As we pray persistently in Jesus' name, in accordance with his views, his plans and his opinions, the enemy is forced to go. Sometimes reluctant, sometimes angry, he is forced to let go. In this, God is wonderfully glorified as he is able to grow his kingdom.

Chapter 8

THREE STEPS FORWARD

The word 'prayer' is one of those generic terms, commonly used to cover any and all styles and methods of communication with God. For the purposes of my own efforts to develop a dynamic, kingdom expanding, private prayer partnership with Christ I have to always remember that this word 'prayer', for my purposes, particularly covers and includes three specific steps of being in touch with God.

Joyfully, my own kingdom prayer partnership grows, continues and expands along these three steps. I find that each one is as vital as the other two.

The first step to take I label 'meeting up' with God. That simply means doing my best to keep on good terms with him. The whole basis of these 'good terms' is possible because of the blood sacrifice of Jesus' death on the Cross. Thankfully, he was raised from the dead and lives now, and my prayer life involves my coming to the Father through him.

This first step is what cements friendship and fellowship with God. It is not what it always used to be – pressing into Father Christmas's hands a wish list for some particular things; it is not asking but simply enjoying him, loving him, thinking about him, how wonderful he is, how amazingly thoughtful, how strong, loving and lovable he is. Talking to him without words – that is the truest worship, thinking how worthy he is of all the best I can possibly bring him.

The foundations of these partnership fellowships are built wholly out of God and his prayer partners being on good terms with each other. I do find that, of necessity, this special time for meeting up has to include some confession on my part of my ignorances and sometimes bad behaviours, and an accepting heart of forgiveness on God's part. This is the only way I can come daily into the relation of fellowship. I always need to apologise for inadequacies and he always re-accepts me into our friendship partnership despite them. This friendship fellowship lies at the base of all prayer partnership. It is the essential breath of the true prayer-giver's life.

For my own benefit, I have labelled the second step of partnership prayer 'Your kingdom come'. I am using those words now in the narrower meaning of asking for something for myself, my family, my friends. These prayers are definite requests to God for something we need.

The whole lives of my family and friends are totally dependent on God's generosity. Everything we need comes from him. Our friendships, any ability and opportunity to make a living, health, having a bit of God's wisdom in difficult circumstances and in all life's swings and roundabouts; help of every kind, financially, bodily, mental, spiritual – all come from God and make it absolutely essential to stay in close touch with him.

I try to keep a constant stream of 'asking prayer' going up, and very often that is wordless prayer. There is a constant return flow of answer (and supply) coming down.

O you who hear prayer, to you all men will come.

Psalm 65:2

God is always alongside, always available. In the moment we turn to him, our prayer is taken on board, listened to, authenticated as coming from him in the first place, because it is God who gives our prayer its value and its character, not our feelings, not our desperation, not our grasp of the language. Prayer accepted by him becomes, by the fact alone that he has accepted it, a true prayer. This is not a formula. Reducing prayer to the level of being just mantra reduces the prayer itself. No, this is a way to rest in his dreams and purposes.

I am always conscious of having to keep the door open between God and me. The doorknob is very much on my side. He unlocked it from his side a long time ago, propped it open and threw the key in the ditch.

The third step is Intercession. True prayer never stops with asking for one's self. It reaches out towards other people as well. The very word 'intercession' implies a reaching out on behalf of someone else. It is standing in as a go-between, a mutual friend, between God and someone who is needing special help. I am finding this step to be so useful in helping the glow of the kingdom to extend to those who have lost touch with God or who never touched him in the first place.

I sense that this third step, intercession, is the spearpoint of prayer. It is the outward drive. It is the effective end of praying. The movements of the first two steps, 'meeting up' and 'Your kingdom come', are upwards and downwards. Step three's foundation in intercession rests on the first two steps of prayer but it is outward reaching.

The first two steps are vital for self, and those around me, and this third type of prayer is for others and for world situations. Times of 'meeting up' and 'Your kingdom come' align us as fully as possible with God. Intercession makes use of that alliance and alignment to see the spreading of the holy glowing kingdom.

In this context, my own intercession time feels like it is the full-flowering plant whose roots and growth lie deep down in the first two steps. It is the form of prayer that helps God in his great love-plan to win a whole planet back into proper order. It helps me to keep this rather simple trilogy of 'three steps of partnership praying' in mind as I try, every day, to work through each of them in turn.

PART TWO

Daily Deepening the Divine Partnership

Chapter 9

A PLACE FOR PRAYER

Firstly, we need to settle on a designated place to start practising our prayer partnership with God. We can pray anywhere, of course. We can pray while out walking the dog, while shopping, watching over the cooking, while sitting in a stationary car trying to drive home after a hard day at the office – everywhere and anywhere. It must be right to pepper our ordinary day with quick prayers in this way. However, all such places and occupations as these are filled with their own distractions and, when we are practising to hear his still small voice of calm, even the most beautiful distractions can be interruptive.

Not only this but we are not very likely to do it on any regular basis unless we decide to go off to some particular and quiet place, shut in alone with God.

After some initial weeks of practice, it began to grow clearer to me that this practice of being a listening prayer partner was becoming more ingrained in my outlook as I go about my normal daily life, with all its jobs, duties and responsibilities. To begin with, however, to learn to listen better – to improve my spiritual hearing – it has been a great help to designate a specific and private place for this practice. To invigorate a meaningful life of prayer partnership I have found it of great importance to discover my own private fig tree.

'How do you know me?' Nathanael asked.

Jesus answered, 'I saw you while you were still under the fig tree before Philip called you' (*John 1:48*, NIV).

It seems that something outside the normal experiences of everyday life had happened to Nathanael under his fig tree. Otherwise it is probably unlikely that Jesus would have mentioned this one particular place. Any other place would do equally as well. Our Lord might have seen him just as easily in his own bedroom, his own garden or in the street. But there was something in his answer that was highly significant to Nathanael.

In those days there were many devout people like him looking for the 'consolation of Israel'; the coming of the King of the Jews. It is easy for me to believe that Nathanael was one of these devout folk, sitting under the fig tree, praying like many other people for the swift coming of the Messiah. When Jesus said to him, 'When you were under the fig tree, I saw you,' Nathanael immediately answered, 'You are the Son of God, you are the King of Israel.'

He was sitting under the tree for this special reason, and not only once. Very probably he had visited this particular spot over the past few months and perhaps even for years. He had been praying for this very thing.

He had selected one special fig tree to be his regular place for prayer. Under that particular tree he would have prayed long and often for Israel's King to come. So when Jesus said, 'When you were under the fig tree, I saw you,' he knew straight away that his often repeated prayers were being answered, thus triggering the response, 'Rabbi, you are the Son of God; you are the King of Israel.'

It is good for growing prayer partnerships to have a secret place of communion like this between them; perhaps at home but perhaps on a mossy bank in the woods, under a big old oak tree, on a grassy spot near a stream, or under a shade-tree that grows alongside a river meandering through a meadow. We can retreat there when the shadows of night begin to fall or when the light of the morning streaks across the sky, and there we can pour out our praise and thanksgiving from the fullness of our hearts.

I find it a delight to have an altar of prayer in a secluded place. There I meet God and tell him all my sorrows, upsets and concerns, and I can tell him, too, about his loving kindness. There I can bathe in the glow of his glory that upholds and sustains both me and those I pray for through all our difficulties in life. There I can worship at his feet.

Every prayer-giver should have a 'fig tree' and often be found under it. Jesus said we should go into a smaller, private place and shut the door before praying. That door he was referring to is important. It shuts out the world and it shuts me in with God's presence. His teaching was: 'Pray to your Father who is in secret....' God is a great deal easier to find here, in this 'shut-in' place, minimising interruptions.

I had to spend time away in a chosen place and on my own, before I found out that I am never alone. Nowadays the more alone I am as far as the world is concerned the less alone I am as far as my relating to God is concerned. I feel that, bit by bit, I grow closer to him through finding a private place for us to focus together.

I have found, too, that a quiet place and time alone with God are absolutely essential as a training ground for my ears. A quiet place softens out the outside noise and gives my spiritual hearing a chance to learn other sorts of sound.

Years ago now, when my wife and I were freshly engaged to be married, in the days before cell phones, I used to phone her in London, UK (where she was studying music). I did this every weekend from a local telephone booth in amongst the local shops and with traffic roaring past across a busy junction.

There were times when it was very difficult to hear her properly on the other end of the phone. I kept saying, 'I can't hear you very clearly, I can't hear you properly. It's the traffic! Could you speak a bit louder?'

Eventually she would say, 'If only you'd shut the door to the phone booth you'd hear me much better!' She was quite right! Not only could I hear her much more clearly but I could still pick up the traffic and people sounds in the background if I needed to. Some of us have got the sources of our hearing sadly confused because our doors have not been closed often enough.

It is too easy to get our human voice and God's voice muddled up in our hearing. We have real difficulty telling them apart, so much so that many of us don't even try to separate them out any more. This difficulty, partly, is with the door. If only we would shut that door we could practise hearing more clearly. Doing this private, shut-away praying had little affect on my hearing while I did it only once or twice a month or when I felt the need for it or had a spare moment. Like most things in life, if we want to get good at anything we need to constantly be getting away for practice.

Let us watch someone for a little while who has worked himself into the true and easy perspective of being a divine prayer partner. This is an ordinary family home where everyday life has a fairly narrow horizon: going shopping with the baby, sewing a torn knee in a worn pair of trousers, cooking, calling a friend, sending text messages and watching social media, doing the family accounts, feeding relentless machines in the factory, driving the tractor, feeding the chickens, doing the household chores and all the rest of the never-ending business of doing – day by day.

This person we are following is carrying out his daily

routines, cheerily, quietly, with some light in his face, a lightness in his step. Where he treads becomes a different place because of the presence of this person with a different spirit.

He is working *in* God – not with him or for him but in him. He is in a private and quiet kingdom prayer partnership with the risen Lord through whom the whole universe was constructed. That is some business partner! He has an unseen Friend at his side. That changes everything.

Here we can watch the private, inner side of life where the greater work is being carried out. It is his quiet slice of time alone with God. It may be early morning before the sun is up and it may be later in the evening – it matters not.

Let us imagine he is leaning on the five-bar field gate at the bottom of his property, looking up reverently into God's face. Christ himself is here, in this peaceful place. The angels are here. This gate opens out into the whole world. For God's prayer partner, its horizon is as broad as the planet itself. Our Lord's presence with him makes it like that.

Running right through this time of silent and private asking are the golden threads of victory in Jesus' name. His whole prayer time is coloured this way. His thoughts are led by the Holy Spirit, back and forth, in and out, across his family, his town, his country, abroad. The tide of prayer sweeps quietly and without resistance, day by day. This is the true Christian life. This man we have been watching is winning souls for Christ and refreshing lives – physically, emotionally, spiritually – both in far-away countries and in close-by places, as truly and as effectively as if he had physically visited each place in turn.

This is part of the Master's plan. The person praying has as broad a horizon as does the Lord he is praying with. Jesus thought in planets, stars, continents and seas. His kingdom prayer partner prays with the same scope. Could this all be too vague? Does he know what is being accomplished? Yes, he does. He knows by the inference of faith.

Worrying about trusting faith in our partnership prayers, we could close our doors and windows in the middle of the day so that no light gets in. A single crack lets in only a single strip of light but that strip betrays a whole world of sunshine outside.

Many of our prayers do get answered, and that is as it should be. Many prayer-givers have assured me that their liturgies or their methods of prayer work as well as any other, but if they use the terms 'method' or 'work', or similar expressions, it suggests that they still look for methods of persuading God to act, having too small a concept of the goodness and greatness of God who simply needs his children to pray in the pattern of his will; to see heaven and earth in one place, full of all his children, living in peace with him and with each other.

Those who apply themselves primarily to allowing their prayer partnership with Christ to grow will wait to hear his voice of direction on how to pray. They receive frequent evidences of changes coming about that have been the subjects of their attentions but they also know very well that these are only the thin line of glory light which has, as it were, crept around the blinds at the edge of the windows. Such evidences tell us of a far fuller shining. We can step back into the everyday workings of the world with our spirits touched with awe and gladness that we can be included in this kingdom life.

Finding a place is one thing, finding the time in our busy lives is a whole other thing.

Chapter 10

TIME TO GROW

It is an uncomfortable thought but there is no such thing as safely standing still in anyone's spiritual life; any one of us not going forwards daily is losing ground. To stay standing still in a place that is comfortable and secure is impossible. If we are not gaining then we are losing.

If we are not rising then we are sinking. If we are not stepping up the rungs of the ladder, we must be slipping back down them; if we don't win, then we will be conquered.

So let us take a step upwards. Lifting our souls above the material world and consciously pondering God himself seems a huge struggle. Such a thing is often beyond the reach of normal experience. God's goal is to get us all back across the divide between kingdom and world and dwell peacefully and happily through life with God himself.

In the story of the Garden of Eden, humans spent time each day in the company of God with no other motives than to seek his company. During Jesus' earthly ministry he spent much time alone with Father God, perhaps from the same motivation. Since those days there have been thousands and thousands of devout people who have followed the same practice. Brother Lawrence wrote:

You might then tell me that I am always saying the same thing. It is true, for this is the best and easiest method I know; and, as I use no other, I advise all the world to it. We must know before we can love. In order to know God, we must often think of him; and when we come to love him, we shall then also think of him often, for our heart will be with our treasure.[1]

For many of us, life is proving to be too busy. Most of us have turned away from God altogether while some, thinking ourselves to be devoutly spiritual people, go multi-tasking. We double up our private time with God with some important worldly activity like baby-sitting the grandchildren in front of their television or being up on the hills walking the dog.

I can only recommend that we would-be prayer partners really do need to set aside some specific and regular time for meeting up with him. How much time? I found my own answer and it is this – enough time to forget what time it is.

My own allocated time to practise is not getting up in the morning at the last possible moment, getting dressed quickly, composing myself in prayer for a few moments to feel easier about a few things or about the day ahead. Neither do I include those quick prayers last thing at night when I am almost ready to drop into bed, often feeling a bit jaded and with sleepy eyelids.

I suppose those short prayer times are, actually, all useful as far as they go. It must always be good to sweeten and sandwich our days with all the prayer time we can squeeze into our crazy schedules.

No, that is not it. I need to set aside time to pray thoughtfully. If that means sacrificing something else to free up the time then so be it. Sacrifice, it seems, is the continual niggle of any busy life. The important thing is often sacrificed to the more important thing. We are all used to managing life like that. It is not such a strange idea. It happens every day.

Jesus often withdrew to lonely places and prayed. It was not at all exceptional for Jesus to go off into the wilderness or up a hill overnight to do this. Why would he need to do it? He was speaking and listening to the Father all day long and, despite being in such constant touch with him, he still felt the need and the joy of more prolonged and quiet time with him. We prayer-givers pray for our own forgiveness but, unlike us, Jesus himself never needed that – yet he needed his prayer time.

The easiest way to concentrate my own mind in this time of prayer, staying focused, is to not let it stray too far from God's presence during the day. I try to keep my mind strictly in the presence of God, frequently thinking about him. As a result, I then find it easier to keep my mind at rest in prayer time, or at least to haul it back from its butterfly wanderings around the flowers of life.

I can see another enormous advantage to this: helping to cultivate a mature judgment about what is going on around me. Otherwise I find my spiritual strength gets frizzled up in worrying about the less important details. There lies the danger of letting slip the greater objective which may, consequently, be left undone altogether.

Those of us who want to be skilled and effective prayer partners with Christ, flowing easily in our prayers under the influence of his will, knowing how to pray easily, simply and forcefully, have to get into the habit of taking some quiet time every day to get away, alone.

They say that practice makes perfect, but perfection, for many of us, is too much to ask. Practice today makes us better tomorrow. How much time I devote to the practice of prayer governs how effective and rewarding my private prayer partnership with the Almighty becomes.

I have met a number of people who would privately think of this sort of prayer time as being in the category of laziness. These are action orientated folks who, at the drop of their leader's hat, would rush to some less well-off community and pour their efforts into such hard work as digging wells, painting schools and building orphanages. My answer to such dismissive thoughts of 'not bothering too much' is to encourage them in their labours all I can. What they do can only be thought of as being marvellous, but we humans can only do as much as we can pray. It is our prayer time that takes the sting out of any influences that might attempt to disturb our progress. It is our prayer partnership that should be allowed to determine our efforts, and our working within that partnership in prayer that greatly increases the effectiveness of that work when it takes place.

The target I aim at? It is a simple and profound daily time and place where I feel that I am actually bathing in Christ's love. This is, indeed, the shelter of the Most High.

Note
[1] Brother Lawrence (c.1605-1691), *The Practice of the Presence of God*, New York, Revell, 1895, Ninth Letter

Chapter 11

MEETING UP

Having chosen a time and chosen a place to do it, I stay quiet and wait, filling that space and time with worship. So, what do I sing? Thankfully for me, worship in the context of strengthening prayer partnerships is the dropping of one's own ideas rather than the singing of church music – if there were countless angels between me and God's throne they might still not be able to filter my singing enough to make it worthy!

My everyday answer to the question of worship is this: hope. The structure of this 'Meeting up' phase of daily prayer, the exercise of which is the major component of building a trusting prayer partnership with Jesus Christ, I find is most easily remembered by working through those four letters of the word H-O-P-E.

I need to approach each one in an 'attitude of gratitude', either with thanksgiving thoughts or often just in silent wonder, love and praise.

The first letter, 'H', stands for Heaven on Earth. This is not a hope in the sense of a little wishful thinking. This is the 'sure and certain hope' in old Church jargon; it is a definite plan awaiting definite fulfilment.

What plan? Reading the biblical creation story, the passages describing the Garden of Eden, we come across a picture in words of a sure and certain hope. It is the idyllic existence that God longs for – all his children living in complete peace and harmony and living with him. It is the life for us that God thinks is 'very good' and the life he would love to have us enjoy on planet Earth.

The garden picture is of a place where life with God is such bliss that heaven and earth are painted the same. They are indistinguishable. Where heaven and earth are one place, Jesus is Lord and every knee shall bow. A new heaven and earth are not lit any more by sun and moon but by the light which is the Son of God himself, the glow of the glory of God.

The point of saying 'Thank you' is that this plan remains the plan to this day, that his overarching desire is to see the plan implemented, all his will today being based in, and coming forth from, that plan.

This place that is both heaven and earth at the same time is the kingdom of God/heaven. It is for the extending of it that we are all called to pray in partnership with Christ: Your kingdom come, your will be done on earth as it is in heaven.

The second letter 'O', sad to say, stands for the opposite. Isaiah the prophet said: "We all, like sheep, have gone astray." God has given us all the ability to make choices and we have turned that gift into the practice of making bad choices. We have turned our backs on God's master-plan for kingdom building. We have walked away and we still walk away even further every day.

Sadly, it goes on. We go on walking away. More and more we convince ourselves that we ourselves are the centre of all things in life, that what we think is what we think and does no longer have to conform or make any allowance for anyone else's opinions. The wisdom of those who went before us is all tossed out of life's window as it never seems to serve our own drive to make our own Self into our own god and king. The fall from God continues.

I suppose this must all make God very sad as it is we, his own family, who dismiss him so readily, preferring to worship other gods of our own making, usually ourselves. We have so much to apologise for. Our hearts should be broken in tune with his.

Thirdly, our stepping through phase 1, the Meeting up phase of prayer, is to know afresh the letter 'P' that stands for the Divine Plan. The kingdom of God/heaven came with Jesus and has not gone away. The first step of 'fixing' the kingdom of heaven here on earth was the cross of Christ. Heaven was nailed to earth through the cross, and vice versa. In his dying, the curtain in the Temple was torn from top to bottom, permanently revealing heaven to all of us. God has broken through again. Heaven is here, it is near and we are all called to partner in its growth with our living Lord.

Last of all in this first prayer step, we give thanks for the letter 'E'. It is the beginning of the two words: 'Even me'. Yes, this partnership includes even me. I accept my total unworthiness in this matter but, as a prayer partner, God has chosen me. I did not choose him, he chose me. That is truly amazing! He has chosen the reader, too!

John Donne wrote:

> This was the fulness of time, when Christ Jesus did come, that the Messiah should come. It was so to the Jews, and it was so to the Gentiles too... Christ hath excommunicated no nation, no shire, no house, no man; He gives none of His ministers leave to say to any man, "thou art not redeemed". He gives no wounded or afflicted conscience leave to say to itself, I am not redeemed.[1]

> So whether you eat or drink or whatever you do, do it all for the glory of God (*1 Corinthians 10:31*, NIV).

This pattern of H-O-P-E, hope, is not meant to be a mantra pattern for evermore but a drill on the recruit's parade ground of the spiritual life by which the would-be prayer partner and change-maker hopes to learn discipline and obedience and, above all, gain a natural affinity to obedience in the field.

Regular set times of meeting up tend to gloriously reshape the prayer-giver as the prayer partnership strengthens. The ways in which this happens are better listed by Roger Williams (1603? – 1683)[2] who wrote:

(1) God's children ought to walk in constant amazement of spirit as to God, His nature, and works.

(2) The glorifying of God is the great work of God's children.

(3) Delightful privacy with God argues strong affection.

(4) Frequent prayer an argument of much of God's Spirit; True prayer is the pouring out of the heart to God; God's children are most in private with God; The prayers of God's people most respect spiritual mercies; God's people wait for and rest in God's answer.

(5) God's people are sensible of their unworthiness.

(6) God Himself is regarded as the portion of His people.

(7) Ready obedience to God.

(8) The patience of God's children under God's hand.

(9) The mournful confession of God's people.

(10) God's people long after God in an open profession of His ordinances.

(11) Their hearts are ready and prepared.

(12) God's people's sense of their own insufficiencies."

It is only on the daily trip to the parade ground to practise these first steps that the recruit prayer partner learns the basics of all there is to learn and the regular exercise of this phase of 'Meeting up' shapes all there is to come. A wholly different, exciting and rewarding prayer life awaits us!

Notes

[1] John Donne (1573-1631), *Works of John Donne*, vol. I, London: John W. Parker, 1839.

[2] In *Experiments of Spiritual Life & Health* (1652).

Chapter 12

PLOUGHING TOGETHER

One of the main purposes of ensuring regular use of the 'Meeting up' time is that, by its own accord, our relationship with God deepens through Jesus to the point where we begin to gain more trust, more awareness of his motives and directions, more assurance that all he asks for in prayer has already been planned, more like-mindedness. This deepening of partnership relationship does not happen by human effort or by study or theology or intellect – it simply happens. It is the most wonderful experience.

Now God and me, in this deepening prayer partnership, can begin to plough the field together! It is not that we shall necessarily begin to hear his voice loudly, deeply and clearly – the beautiful and realistic effects of regularly practising 'Meeting up' is that our like-mindedness grows sharper and, as it does so, his interpretations of events around us become more focused in our own conscience and understanding of them. Thus it is, without thought or discussion or judgement, that we naturally grow more obedient to that specific call to pray and that specific line of prayer.

It often seems important just to keep out of his way! I so well remember, at the very start of my public ministry, being in a difficult situation that I had no idea how to handle. I found it most difficult and very embarrassing. As I secretly cried 'Help!' the thought came immediately to mind, 'Take your feet off the ground and I can carry you.'

In giving up all attempts to find wisdom to solve the situation, in standing waiting for someone else to do something or to say something deep and profound, waiting too long to remain comfortable, the answer came – not through me but through a complete stranger to the issue. God had intervened through someone else and won through because I stood aside.

Waiting for us is the thrill of having our prayer relationship with God revitalised and deepened into significant kingdom action. We can look forward to this, not because it might or might not yield better results but for the thrill of being included in the home team, in partnership in God's masterplan to bring all his children home into his kingdom. The passing thrill of scoring a few crowd-cheering points for the local team, once or twice a season, in no way compares with the deepest ongoing satisfaction in being an accepted and valued member of the national squad!

Having spent a regularly recurring time in Step 1, it is time to enter into Step 2, holding all the while that thrill of being a chosen member of the 'national kingdom squad' rather than hoping to score the odd point now and again in the village team. What, then, can we be walking into?

Analogies never quite seem to work very well in the Christian context. They are not spiritually perfect! Of course, the parables of Jesus always work perfectly, but analogies that are from a mostly human source so often have in-built flaws. Notwithstanding, here goes with a pair of carthorses!

We begin with a scene from long ago rural England, long ago before the raucous coming of the combustion engine, when the sights and sounds of the countryside left the watcher securely at home in a quieter heart. Let us exercise our imaginations and lean on a nearby gatepost.

Not a single grey cloud billows above us across a hot

blue sky. Not a breeze can swish the birch branches or brush the clouds away. All is quiet, all is calm. There is only the rhythmic plodding of horses' hooves, the jangle of horse brasses and the clanking of heavy chinking chains pulling a plough across a stubborn stubble field.

Birds and butterflies inhabit the hedgerows around us and flocks of flies buzz around the horses' eyes and over their backs, snapped away by flapping ears, shaking heads, flicking tails. The ploughshares behind the team bite deep, turning the ground, filling the landscape with the promise of fruitfulness to come.

Here are two horses driving, steadily heaving, very different from each other. The one that would draw our watchful eye is much the bigger, the stronger and far, far wiser than the other. This one is on the inside of the two, the anchor holding the pair steady as they round the corners of life, the ends of the furrows.

The other, tripping and skipping around its friend, is much younger, far less experienced in the art of tilling seed-hungry fields. This one is unsteady against the older leading horse, sometimes bubbling over with enthusiasm, sometimes pushing on too much, sometimes dancing sideways to avoid the bigger stones, sometimes holding back noisily, surrendering to waves of indifferent reluctance and the snickering advice from inquisitive horses across the hillside. So the two plough on together somehow – teacher and learner, the patient, wise old professor and the immature, skittish and self-willed student.

But these two are linked together, strapped close for the work to hand. Across their shoulders (around their hearts) lies a strong, unbendable leather harness, a yoke especially made to fit them both. This weighty leather bolster would seem at first heavy, blister bursting and cumbersome to the watching eye, and yet it feels so light to the horses because it has been formed to fit so comfortably to each neck and shoulder in turn.

As they travel purposefully together for as long as there is daylight, up and across that field, and another field and yet another one, the younger, smaller horse slowly but surely begins in weariness to learn the way. He feels and listens and reacts rather than make his own decisions. He senses the close master horse's movements, sensing them through the leather harness against his shoulders.

And thus, in time, the student grows calmer, more steady and quieter in his movements, concentrating less on the daunting volume of uncut acreage – not on the watchers or the disturbing flittering of the flies around his face or the weighty plough coming on behind them nor the continual straining effort in the pulling. His focus is on the master, sensing his thinking, having his own spirit tuned to the master horse's guiding. Their partnership teamwork is building.

Since starting out on the practice of kingdom partnership, it has always been a practical help to me to imagine the master horse as being God and the young, more inexperienced one as being myself. In which case I have seen the harness, tying the two in together, as being rather like the action of the Holy Spirit. My entire prayer life had been spent in the adjoining pasture, leaning over the gate and admiring the ploughing. Now I was being called to jump the fence and slip my shoulders into the harness.

In the beginning of anyone's learning, the teamwork is very clumsy! The Master's will applied to the restoring of creation is unbendable. The younger horse may see what he believes might be obstacles up ahead, stepping to right and to left to avoid them, stepping high over the bramble thorns, leaning more heavily into the harness across more rocky soil and hanging back when tired, hoping to be carried on by his work partner's energy, and to catch his breath. If the learner is not moving in exactly the same way as the Master then we might sense a very jerky and unsatisfying piece of teamwork.

I am keenly aware that so much of my past Christian prayer life was filled with attempts to invoke the Master to follow the thoughts and the workings of the junior prayer-giver! Again, we would-be partners may consider it a most spiritual thing to watch to see how the Master steps. First this foot, and then that foot, and then the others follow like this and like that. In studying the Master's movements, as if learning a ritual, we hopefully learn to march in step. Even worse, we sometimes wait for breaks in our schedule and peer over the nearest hedge to watch how other teams of horses do the ploughing in the hope of learning technique from them at a more comfortable distance.

Divine partnership life is not like this – one straight step followed by another. The Master may all the time be intent on ploughing the field but, in the doing, will need to be so sensitive to the ground beneath his feet and move, every inch by every inch, accordingly.

So we don't need to pre-learn to mimic the Master's movements, or anyone else's, to learn a divinely choreographed ballet of prayer. We prayer-givers can become more sensitive to every inflection of movement as it happens, as the Master senses and decides the best minute by minute approach to what lies underfoot. .

The junior member of this working relationship has no need to copy the way the Master lifts and steps his feet or holds his head, but desperately needs to appreciate the same sense of mood, voice – every aspect of his big brother's approach to the task in hand. As such sensitivity develops, the junior relies less and less on gifts of prophetic words and pictures as these are easily bent and coloured by the workings of the human nature.

Instead, more and more as he practises this sensitivity,

he gains oneness with the Master's detailed godly wisdom. In this way the operation at hand becomes smoother and smoother, more and more in harmony with God.

'.....far above all rule and authority, power and dominion, and every name that is invoked, not only in the present age but also in the one to come. And God placed all things under his feet and appointed him to be head over everything for the church, which is his body, the fullness of him who fills everything in every way' (Ephesians 1:21–23).

It is not for us to determine whether or not the ploughing becomes more effective, straighter, deeper, more potentially fruitful. Our best interest is to please God by playing our part best in the Master's desire for harmonious working with his children.

The regular practice of Step 1, Meeting up, is the bedrock on which a growing prayer partnership may flourish. The flower has begun to open.

Chapter 13

YOUR KINGDOM COME

While enjoying giving glory to God as described, expressing thanks for his recovery-plan and for its major step of implementation through the cross. I would now need to know who to pray about and how to pray so that I can fill my role in the partnership as an input port into the world, for heaven's restoring and rehabilitating graces.

Anyone now going on to this second phase, the one I call 'Your Kingdom Come', invites God into those situations the Holy Spirit prompts them towards. In the main, this is initially someone in my group of friends and family. Prayer flows through our individual personalities and these are the ones we feel most strongly about, the ones most close to us – our personal mission field.

Keen as I might be to allow God's direct involvement in a problem, I cannot risk pulling up any spiritual blinkers and blocking God's other possibilities. What could they be? I must always wait a while to listen out for the object needing specific prayer, simply because we are such complicated beings! We may not be getting better quickly from an illness for a number of reasons, and which one am I to pray into? The answer will be different in every single case because we are all different.

Some of those I want to pray for may be physically very poorly – but through conditions brought on by emotional depression or by self pity. Others need medical and some surgical help, and some need emotional support. Some have grown to live in their poor conditions; some, emotionally insecure, seek any kind of attention. Some behave badly through slack upbringing, and some have mental issues that might lead to anti-social activity, while some have simply caught something nasty – and so on, and so on. The symptom might well have been self-diagnosed or medically diagnosed, but behind it could lie a large variety of things that are pinning the condition in place.

In private prayer I try to wait in silence for instruction from above on which 'trapdoor' to open for his restoration to flow through. His answer always remains a secret between us as I could be wrong. In secret prayer, kept to ourselves, this sort of error causes no damage. If, then, accepting the possibility of an error seems the right thing to do, back I go again into my prayer partnership for another quiet meeting on the subject – as the Eden story relates, 'in the cool of the day'.

Thinking of a friend or a member of the family can be extremely painful in itself. We ourselves can be physically and mentally beaten down by life-threatening disease or accident, or other events that leave us feeling desperate for help. Practising my own prayer partnership with Jesus, I find it far easier to approach my own troubles, and those of family and friends, in holy simplicity. That phrase means watching those aspects of the trouble that are close at hand and not worrying about dangers which lurk off at a distance, near or far. It is easy to imagine such things to be forests when they might only be trees on the hill top. Raising our view of this to focus on the forests, we might step across on to a wrong prayer path, or even trip and injure ourselves on rocks along the way.

As a prayer partner to the Lord I stand in line with countless angels and countless other prayer-givers. I simply belong to a private army whose commander in chief knows all things and directs all things.

Although someone needing God's involvement in their lives may come to my notice, I cannot assume total responsibility for God's intervention. I am merely one in an army. Individual soldiers do not win battles, it is the General who does it! He may not even require my involvement at all, as all we soldiers have different personalities and ways of looking at things through which he may wish to work.

Then again, knowing all there is to know about everything, God must be left to decide his own best approach to the situation. This might be through one of that troubled person's friends, a family member, through someone with medical or psychological training, an unknown shopper's passing comment, a church minister, another member of the same church. Who knows? The answer to that is this: God knows and God can organise it.

Before I started out on my own journey into prayer partnership with God, I regarded prayer as a way to enlist God's help as one option among the suggested list above. If one did not work, the other might! My discovered truth along the road is that all things have been placed under Jesus' feet, that he is over all things, and that our prayers, righteously guided, allow for the right trapdoor to be opened to allow grace to flow in.

So I wait for instruction. I have never to my knowledge been so blessed as to hear the audible voice of God but, through the daily practice of Meeting up with him, I am beginning to discern the prayer approach to the problem required of me. When sifting through all the possibilities I can think of, the specific prayer direction comes to me in the form of a quickly rising sense of excitement, of absolute knowledge, of trust in God.

However, I am thrilled every day by this thought of a working, achieving, kingdom-spreading prayer partnership with God the Father through Jesus, a developing one-mindedness that keeps God's partners on track, making sure they only ever pray along his specific lines. Some are mystified by this. Some are bored. Some are impatient to go on further. Some get excited, some reassured, some are angry when their theological boats get rocked. Some just want to see God perform miracles. Some keep him on standby in the wings of life in case they need him, and some would love a full-on working partnership with him.

What did I ever imagine would be in it for me? There once came a time in my prayer imagination when I was standing knee-deep in the cool waters of an estuary, some three feet from the bank, roasting in the afternoon heat on my back and the reflecting rays of the sun coming off the surface of the water onto my arms and face.

I felt a sense of sinking in my heart as I allowed my gaze to drift up and down the river bank in front of me; away to my left and down to my right there were plants wilting and dying in the direct glare of the sun, the parched heat and the dry soil. So near and yet so far – rows of plants only a few inches from the water's edge and yet drying out and dying out in the heat of the day. So it is to have compassion for those who suffer at home and across the world. We pray for them in the only way we know how. I bent down, scooping my cupped hands up from between my knees and splashing the nearest plants with the reviving, cooling water they needed in order to survive. I seemed to do this a hundred, if not a thousand times, while my back felt as though it were breaking – and I was simply not satisfied with the results.

Eventually, as tears of exasperation began to flow down and mix themselves with the handfuls of water, the nearest plants began slowly to develop darker brown patches of earth around them and, in time, some – not enough – seemed to recover slightly. I stood up to stretch my muscles, aching from the work, wiping my sleeve across my streaming forehead. I glanced up and down the bank again at the acres of suffering plants, and returned to my labours. Digging out my watch from a pocket, I looked at it quickly. Another two hours or so and I could go home, secure in the knowledge that I had done my best for another day. I swallowed down the thought that I would most likely have failed many more plants than I had been able to rescue, but then how could I be expected to do everything around here? After all, I am only one among many. I could not see any other colleagues from my spot in the river, but I was sure they must be around somewhere.

As far as I could see, I was doing the job aright. I was metaphorically standing in the river of God's reliable, rescuing grace, and doing my little bit by praying for the ones nearest to me through that grace. This is all we can do. Anyway, in a little while I straightened up again, stretching my shoulders backwards to ease the muscle ache in them. Someone was coming closer. From away to my right, through the heat haze, there emerged a rider and a shimmering white horse clopping along the riverside path towards me. I could use his coming to wait and rest on the off-chance of some conversation.

Hoof beat by hoof beat, he slowly came nearer and then, as he reached me, he reined in his horse and leaned slowly forward, face turned towards me and forearms resting on the pommel. The broad brim of his hat obscured much of his face in shadow.

'Good afternoon, sir,' I offer.

'May I ask what you're doing?' he enquires of me.

'I was out for a walk along here this morning,' I told him, 'and caught sight of all these lovely plants and flowers up and down the river bank. They're doing very badly in the heat. They were suffering and dying and yet all they're doing is just being here! I wanted to help so I climbed into the river and began to scoop water. I have no bucket or hose, only my hands. I suppose that's alright because it's the water that does the refreshing, not me! Now my back is getting the better of me so I'll stop soon and go home for a rest!'

Without taking his eyes off me for a moment, he raised himself upright again in the saddle and said, 'Follow me!'

'Who are you?' I asked him in turn. I was tired and hot and dirty and I wanted to go home. If I was going to follow someone at this endpoint of such a dusty and exhausting day, heaven only knows why. I needed to know what I was going to let myself in for.

The rider waved a hand along the far estuary bank, all the way along in one direction and back along the near bank.

'All this is mine.' He was smiling fondly at the whole vista of browns, greens and blues in front of him as he said this. 'The river is mine and the ground to either side is mine. Where the estuary comes from is mine and where it flows into the sea is mine. The air above it is mine, and the plants are mine. Follow me and I'll show you something.'

So I did. It seemed uncomfortable to be carried along like this; I was right to do what I had been doing; I was right to be where I was, and now it was right to go home. I took a step of faith. This was against my better judgement but I took the step, nevertheless. His words seemed to want to direct my path.

I climbed and slipped unsteadily back up the bank and rolled down my trouser legs. I slipped my socks and shoes on again as the rider applied his heels to the flanks of the white horse, who set off at a steady pace, the horseman never looking back to see if I was following. I was. So we went on for a little while, no one speaking. I was finding strength and support in the sweltering heat by pacing my footsteps in the rhythm of the horses' hooves. Straight on we went for over a mile, turning to the right as we followed the line of the river around a wide bend to a place where it widened out even further, between the wooded hillsides that held a boathouse at their feet.

'There,' he pointed out to me, 'in that boathouse is a gift for you. You have worked hard on my river and you have worked well with my flowers but now I have a reward for you. It's my pleasure to give it to you. Enjoy it and you will learn something.'

Intrigued, I climbed down the wooded path until I reached the boat shed door, left unlocked, and lightly ajar in its own welcome. Inside was a sight that took my breath away. Lying there quietly, waiting for me, was the sleekest and most beautiful speedboat I had ever seen. It had two mighty motors mounted on its stern and the painter was cast loose in readiness for me.

I turned to wave my thanks to the rider, but of course he had gone. The main boat shed doors were lying open onto the water. Both engines roared and leaped into life at my touch. The bow lifted to the wooded banks on the other side and the stern sank as the propeller blades bit deep.

Managing to stay upright under the forces of acceleration, I threw the tiller to one side and we were away up river, white water boiling behind me, wind playing with my hair and keeping my face cool as the evening sun burned down. We roared very quickly up river until it seemed right to turn the boat around.

The engines softened and the bow turned, only to rise again towards the sky as I let the engines have their freedom. Soon we were racing past the boat shed again on our way downstream and all thoughts of strain and stress were gone. Anxiety had left me and my aching shoulders were beginning to recover strength after the day's toil.

All was well with the world. I opened the throttles as far as they would go — this was the stuff that any child's adventure is made of!

When the way ahead appeared empty, safe and clear for a moment, I turned to look behind and thrilled with the sight of it. The blue-white waves, one issuing from either side of the stern, broadened and widened out behind me as I sped along, until, a long way behind me, they reached the bank. This wall of water was quite high enough to fling itself far up the dry earth bank — and the deluge completely swamped every plant, every struggling and suffering flower and weed alike, almost up as high as the rider's footpath and certainly for the entire length of the river.

To complete my joy for them all, the other wave soaked and nearly drowned the opposite bank to exactly the same extent.

How much effort had I by now put in to saving the plants? None at all. All I had done was enjoy myself in taking the fullest advantage of the gift of the boat and access to the river.

Then it slowly began to dawn on me – effective prayer will never be a function of how hard I work at it or how theological or devout I may sound. It will be the fallout of my living in, enjoying to the full, a prayer partnership with the Divine in his kingdom. The dawning of this truth was stunning — I had never even heard a whisper of it before.

I cut the engines and we glided gently to a halt in the quiet of the river afternoon. There was no sign of the rider anywhere along either bank. I could only fall to my knees in the bottom of the boat and thank him for this clear revelation. I would never have imagined that I could have watered the banks in that dramatically effective way. He had shown me the gift of his cross and given me access to and authority in the kingdom. He had taught me that the foundation of all I need to do is to thank him and praise him and enjoy my kingdom living, and the plants around me would in their turn receive in my wake.

"But all this is too easy!" I shout towards the wooded river bank in the hope that the rider might hear me, but there was no answer. His silence seemed like the deep and contented acceptance of heaven.

The lesson of the estuary vision is clear – the regular and consistent healing of the world's ills is not best achieved through choosing a particular methodology, nor by choice of ritual, nor by deeds and actions, nor even necessarily by the non-stop application of 'getting' prayers. It will not have escaped the reader's attention that consistent results by any of these means is often nothing short of grinding hard work, if indeed such a successful ministry of prayer is possible at all!

I had been shown something that I badly needed to know, before any prayer partnership in line with kingdom principles could really work through me to any sizeable and reliable degree. I had seen that a divine prayer partnership is not a social or a church duty or a drudge after all, it is the natural outworking of an everyday God follower. It is the natural kingdom dynamic that results from the bold and full sharing of the good news of the cross.

Putting it another way, messing about in the river up to my knees was a picture of a minister trying his best to disseminate grace. Driving up and down in the speedboat is a picture of a disciple enjoying his true kingdom role, that of partnering with God himself in the work of spreading the heart of his kingdom. The true prayer-giver is someone who simply enjoys praising and giving thanks for all that Jesus has done and lives in the kingdom to the utmost – and the world changes in his wake.

The revealed secrets of this kingdom are interlaced throughout the structure of the New Testament. It is neither exclusively mine nor my colleagues' nor anyone else's; it belongs to each one of us who knows they are called to partake of it.

I have sometimes heard it said that even if there were no rights or wrongs assumed about the way we do any kind of prayer, the church, created by Jesus to further the work of the kingdom of God, could always be judged by the extent to which we are successful in advancing that kingdom. I can now see that this idea comes from a misunderstanding of what is meant by the 'kingdom of God'.

The kingdom itself is not something to be 'furthered' or 'built on' solely by our efforts. It is something which we are asked to realise as being here already, in the life and work of Jesus. It is something that we who believe in Christ should not be actively trying to grow and stretch and give away, as I had been trying to do in the river up to my knees. It is something to inherit and enter into. The role of the church, in these matters, is hardly to persuade the world how it might be a better place than it is at present, but to draw a curtain aside from it, to reveal something that is already here.

Now that I have waited in the prayer time and picked up what I have heard in my spirit, I need to check that what I am asking for fits both of two categories: firstly, that my prayer is a righteous one; and, secondly, does it fall in line with the master-plan for restoration? For the would-be prayer-giver starting out in their prayer partnership with God, these two questions are easily answered.

Chapter 14

RIGHTEOUS PRAYER, RIGHTLY PRAYING

It is here, when stepping into kingdom partnership prayer, that I need to pray aright for friends and family but who should I be praying for and what makes it a *righteous* prayer? If it isn't a righteous prayer then God simply won't be able to look at it, so this determination is most important. What prayer is righteous? What prayer will God support with power?

The question of who to pray for is easily answered as the subject of my love and holy attentions will usually be, but not always, someone already within my personal mission field, i.e. those people whom God places around each of us in life.

Almost without fail, I have three things to check out first; my own diagnostic-giving spirit, my fine tuning in to God and his plans, and my own deeper motives in asking. If all three are righteous then I feel I can approach God through Jesus, my prayer partner, with the problem held out in my hands.

After all, I am forever reminding myself, God can only do what God wants to do, so checking on these three possible interferences will keep me fairly smoothly in prayer partnership with him. Although all righteous prayer originally emanates from God, it is so easy to let our own motives disrupt them. When our prayer lives continue in this world as if only God and ourselves are in it, then our hearts in prayer will never be nudged sideways by any thoughts that could misdirect them.

Firstly, before I turn to praying, I find I need to be constantly checking on my own diagnostic-giving spirit. My natural tendency, quite common I believe, is to want to diagnose at every level. I am often too tempted to dwell on any difficulty of a friend or a member of my own family and tease out, in my own mind, precisely what is causing the problem and therefore, in some detail, how I would like to see God handle it.

However, life's damages are usually far more complicated than we might, at first glance, suppose them to be. There might have been a range of incidents which separately, or even rolled together, might have caused the damage to occur. Multiplying again the possibilities, there may be a number of symptoms of the damage which, should we trouble ourselves with it, might occur on the diagnostic lists of a hundred different complaints. To multiply the multiple possibilities yet again, there may be a whole number of routes that God might choose to take through the resources under his feet to reach a place where his riches can be imparted into the injury.

To specifically request that God move to set aright a particular symptom, through a specific root and via a specific route, closes countless other doors to numberless other possibilities as our expectation of God coming along his own track is narrowed down by our inadequate wisdom and experience. As an example to avoid, I confess my own poor handling of my wife's recent household accident.

She had slipped sideways and off balance while standing on a stool to reach the top of a curtain pole. For some reason, the top of her head met sharply with the top corner of the kitchen wall cupboard, cutting the skin and leading to much bleeding. She was very shaken. The following day she felt dizzy and slightly upset in her stomach and began to have a tightening sensation around her head, together with a sharper headache. This, a day later, grew into a tingling, post-dentist kind of feeling running down the side of her face, as far as her jaw, down the same side as the injury in her scalp.

What to pray for when this happened? Immediately I had begun to make lists in my mind. So had she. We'd be better off not daring to compare notes! Medically, anatomically, judging from those symptoms, anything could have happened. We could just have waited for it all to pass or we could have rushed to hospital. She might just have injured a nerve with some mild concussion, but then it could have been something far worse. Both our imaginations had been running riot. There had come the moment to choose a course of action. Which would God prefer? Hospital? Doctor's surgery? Pharmacy? Friends who were once nurses? Friends who weren't? On the other hand we might just wait overnight and take stock of things in the morning. Which way to move?

Thus continued my whirling diagnostic frame of mind, like the blades of a passing helicopter, without realising that in deciding and then praying for one thing I would be opening only one portal for the Lord, the door of my own human choice, limiting divine grace to that one humanly defined aspect as I was discounting the other divine options. No one else knew of the accident.

Eventually I subsided back into my burgeoning prayer partnership in simple trust that God knows much better than I do how the human body works, what precise injury might have occurred, and which was the best route for him to take through all his resources. I had decided then to leave it all to him and relax into the recognition that all we really wanted was to be mended by any means to hand – his hand. After talking the problem over with the Master in his grace, I settled my heart to watch for any opening doors. My wife's damage was solved within twenty-four hours.

Secondly, there is the question of fine tuning into God's plans. This need for harmonic preparation was confusing and full of doubt to start with, but still grows a little easier as I travel slowly but steadily along the road by which I grope my way towards a more harmonious prayer partnership.

Having determined who I should pray for this day, I can easily make absolutely certain that I am asking for something which would indeed be within the stream of his will. One way I use through this 'self editing' deliberation is to match, in my mind, the sufferer's need (as I might perceive it, rightly or wrongly) with those particular things which Christ himself has already won for us on the cross. They are his gifts of grace revealing heaven's riches so they must surely be part of his will to redeem and repair. The list of these gifts is all-encompassing. The power of God lies in this message:

For the message of the cross is foolishness to those who are perishing, but to us who are being saved it is the power of God (1 Corinthians 1:18).

The kingdom has the cross at its centre, the message of which is the power source for all miracle working. The kingdom atmosphere is filled with the gifts of Calvary — those heavenly riches won by Jesus on the cross in sufficient measure for all who will receive them. All these gifts are already present in the kingdom — it's for us to breathe in the atmosphere. Picking the appropriate gift ensures harmony with his will as he went to the ultimate trouble to gain them for us. Such riches as these are the gifts of Calvary:

(1) Peace

Surely he took up our griefs and carried our sorrows, yet we considered him stricken by God, smitten by him, and afflicted. But he was pierced for our transgressions, he was crushed for our iniquities; the punishment that brought us peace was upon him and by his wounds we are healed.

Isaiah 53:4–5

Jesus bore the punishment that was due for our transgressions and all our iniquities, our acts of rebellion. All the punishment for every act committed by every member of the entire Adamic race was brought onto Jesus. The blessing now available, the alternative, is summed up in the word 'peace'. In place of punishment there is peace, reconciliation and pardon.

(2) Healing

He has taken all our pains and carried all our sicknesses and by his wounds we are healed. He bore our griefs and he carried our sorrows, the result being that by his wounds we are healed. He was physically wounded so that we might be healed. The Hebrew words for griefs and sorrows mean, literally, sicknesses and pain. We can now exchange healing through his wounds for our physical sicknesses.

(3) Abundance

Deuteronomy 28 lists all the curses that are due as punishment for rebellion and the blessings to cancel them out. (See Deuteronomy 28:47f.)

These curses all added up to a state of total and absolute poverty, and that curse came onto Jesus, too. He was hungry, not having eaten for almost twenty-four hours. He himself said "I thirst ." He was naked – the soldiers had taken all his clothes for themselves, casting lots for his seamless robe. Jesus was left hanging without a stitch of clothing, and it had to be so. He was totally bereft of everything, in want of all things, a picture of total poverty, exhausting the curse.

Jesus who was rich with heaven's riches became poor on the cross so that we might in turn be rich. This is the outpouring grace of God.

(4) His righteousness (See 2 Corinthians 5:21)
Jesus, who knew no sin 'became' sin for us. He did this for us so that we might be made the righteousness of God.

(5) Immortality (see Hebrews 2:9)
Jesus, our substitute, tasted every person's death – the punishment due to each one of us because the wages of sin is death. Jesus died as our representative, on our behalf. He has tasted death so that we might have life – that is to say divine, eternal life.

(6) A new nature (see Romans 6:6)
Our old human nature is to be crucified because Jesus was crucified. The rebellion, stubbornness and self-will we have received from Adam is put to death. Jesus, who was himself sinless, identified himself with us on the cross, experienced death for us, and experienced separation from the Father so that we could know God as *our* Father. Again, in Romans 5:19 we read that through the obedience of the one man the many will be made righteous.

All these gifts of Calvary are freely available and come near, as we honour God with thank-offerings for them and for Jesus and his redeeming work on the cross.

Thirdly, I need to check my deepest motives, not with God but with my conscience. The question is this: why am I praying for this situation? Is it really for their good or for mine in any way? Let us allow two examples to make this as clear as we can.

I met a minister once who told me that he prayed diligently for more people to become members of his church. After a number of years those prayers had still never, in his oversight of that congregation, been fulfilled to any significant degree.

When I asked him what his reasons were for praying for

such a thing, he replied to the effect that it was for their soul's good. He wanted everyone in his neighbourhood to become Christians. He emphasised baptism as the key to church membership, and that consequent and subsequent church membership and attendance would eventually lead to everlasting life.

The idea of the sacrament of Baptism in itself being the key to salvation might raise quite a few ecclesiastical eyebrows, so his motives for such praying were gently pursued until a more truthful admission was also made. Layered in underneath all his other and more righteous motives, then there surfaced a covert and desperate need to improve his church's finances, to fund certain projects and to maintain the building in a more permanent manner. The righteous part was an ache to see souls saved but the prayer might have been soiled by wrong motives.

On another occasion, I heard a rumour that a certain lady's somewhat abusive husband had decided he did not want her children around the house at Christmas – children from her first marriage. They should have to be parted, he considered, from their mother and deposited with another relative. I found the news to be heartbreaking. Children of their young age should not, I reasoned, be separated from their mothers at Christmas. What must that mother's agony be like? I felt an urgent and painful need to pray, and chose abundance from the list of the gifts of Calvary – abundance of relationships. Before praying, I remembered to carry out my three checks and stumbled on the third one, my underlying motives for prayer. Having talked this over with my divine prayer partner with due reverence, I realised that I was praying out of my own hurt and that my own heartache was actually at the basis of my intended prayer request. So I abandoned all to him for his own solution, knowing absolutely that the best would happen.

The following morning we discovered from the lady herself that no such divisive decision had been made after all. Her own mother had come to stay for Christmas and all was well. The family would be together.

Here is an interesting comment:

There is, indeed, or at least there hath been, much good, useful good, done by others, on various convictions and for various ends; but there is one flaw or other in all they do. Either superstition, or vain-glory, or selfishness, or merit, or one thing or other, gets into all the good that is done by unholy persons, and brings death into the pot; so that although it may be of some use in particulars, unto individual persons, in some seasons, it is of none unto the general good of the whole.

He that bears the likeness of God, and in all that he doth acts from that principle, he alone is truly useful, represents God in what he doth, and spoils it not by false ends of his own.[1]

Note
[1] John Owen (1616-1683), in A Discourse Concerning Holy Spirit (1674), included in *Works of John Owen*, (Johnson and Hunter, 1852).

Chapter 15

FAITH ARISES

Then Moses summoned Joshua and said to him in the presence of all Israel, "Be strong and courageous, for you must go with this people into the land that the LORD swore to their ancestors to give them, and you must divide it among them as their inheritance. The LORD himself goes before you and will be with you; he will never leave you nor forsake you. Do not be afraid; do not be discouraged."

Deuteronomy 31:7f., NIV

I have often heard people wishing for and praying for a more trusting faith. When I have listened carefully and got down to the bottom of it all, it frequently was not more trusting faith at all they wanted but a more effective way of making it easier for God to change the situation they are praying for. This is more like trying to change from faith to sight. Trusting faith does *not* say: This is good for me so it must have come from God.

Rather than thinking of this from that quite common angle, it seems more likely that Moses and Joshua were thinking at the time: God sent it, so it must be good for us.

This latter view wholly depends, of course, on the prayer-giver knowing full well that what they are faced with is, in reality, a gift from God. Then faith, when walking in the dark with God, only attracts him to hold our hand more tightly.

Faith is to the soul what life is to the body. Prayer is to faith what breath is to the body. How a person can live and not breathe is past my comprehension, and how a person can believe and not pray is past my comprehension too.[1]

There is something here which is very familiar and yet is too often misunderstood. It is that prayer has to be *in faith*. It is where rising faith meets descending grace that the kingdom gains elbow room to move on this planet. It is here that God's intentions move toward fulfilment.

I must note here that faith, in the context of partnership praying, is not believing that God *can*, it is believing that he *will*. All righteous prayer emanates from God, and he asks me to talk to him about a small piece of it. And he will do it! I remind myself of this talk-it-over, trapdoor-opening partnership arrangement, after having prayed, by talking to him in this vein: 'Father, thank you for Jesus and that, through him and our prayer partnership together, we can move mountains. Thank you, then, that what looks to me like a mountain is not merely moveable, it is about to move.'

Then I feel comfortable getting up, leaving my private place and going about any other jobs and duties, thinking to myself: that business of mountain-moving is all organised.

It always pays to watch out for favourable results. Another day, if I have not yet seen a breakthrough, I have to take a careful look at the scene in question. Very often there are hundreds of little circumstances that contribute to the original problem needing the Spirit's grace, and which route to take must always be left to God to choose. He is far more strategically 'gifted' than I am. I then find myself going back over and over again, repeating the prayer in an attitude of gratitude and saying to myself as I leave my prayer time: That matter is most definitely on the run.

This seeming repetition should never be considered a

matter of going back into heaven's courts again and again, to pester and persuade God, to wake him up or to get him to move. I battle on in prayer because prayer can be the deciding factor in any good versus evil conflict. Each prayer is another blow right between the enemy's eyes. Such repetition is the business of beating a path for God, of making such paths straight for him.

Does every praying person I have ever met have a trusting faith of that kind? No, and it is easy to tell why. The trusting faith that believes that God is about to do what we ask is not something born in a hurry. It does not come about through some sudden theological or spiritual revelation. It is not brought into being by taking God for granted or as a reaction to peer influence. It usually is not born at the sight of a miracle or in a noisy crowd. We can know, however, where that faith will be born and go on growing stronger. Trusting faith begins its life in any of us who takes the time off regularly with God, listening to his voice and his Word.

Such resolute trust has three simple characteristics by which we can recognise it – and it is not worked up by us but out of its own nature:

1. Trust is intelligent because it seeks. It finds out what God is wanting to do in any given situation.

2. It fits our lives into God's will, not the other way around. Too many of us claiming to trust God are simply trusting he will give us what we want when we want it. True trust moulds us into his life, it does not try to mould his life into ours! That would be the wrong way round.

3. Trust keeps an eye out for the result of prayer so that, when it sees that gift, it can give high thanks in the heavenly places. We pray, "Your kingdom come." Watching for the kingdom coming is not about getting what we want but being what he wants us to be.

God wants us to be willingly trustful in him.

If the vision tarries, wait for it, it will not delay it will surely come (Habakkuk 2:3).

Note
[1] J. C. Ryle (1816-1900), *A Call to Prayer*, published as a pamphlet, American Tract Society, 1867,

PART THREE

The Work and Influence of a Kingdom Ambassador

Chapter 16

THE BIBLE

The deceit, the lie of the devil, consists of this, that he wishes to make man believe that he can live without God's Word. Thus he dangles before man's fantasy a kingdom of faith, of power, and of peace, into which only he can enter who consents to the temptations; and he conceals from men that he, as the devil, is the most unfortunate and unhappy of beings, since he is finally and eternally rejected by God.[1]

This helpful hint on partnership praying deserves a re-emphasising injection into everyone's personal habits every day. It is that we should give the Bible its proper place in prayer. Prayer is not simply a matter of talking at God about what we want. It is listening first, then talking. The listening bit has to come before the talking bit!

Exercising the art of prayer, allowing an effective prayer partnership to develop, through which God can work, needs three organs, an ear, a tongue and a pair of eyes. In order of use, I first need an ear to hear what God says, then secondly a tongue to talk with, then thirdly my sense of awareness to keep watching out for the result.

Bible study (albeit private reading time at home) is the *listening* side of all this. The grand purposes of God come in through the ears, metaphorically speaking, passing through our hearts where they take on the flavour of our own personality. Then they pass out of us through our tongue in the form of prayer – back to God.

God is always speaking but, even where there may be someone wanting to listen, the sounds of this world too easily smother the sound of his voice in our souls.

The Bible makes this process much easier. God himself speaks in these books. That puts the Bible in a library by itself, quite apart from all other books. Studying it carefully, looking not for the details with which to judge others, but for a glimpse of God's great strategies for the recovery of creation – and that is the whole point. To operate in this world as a really effective working prayer partner in the kingdom means that we have to become more and more finely tuned, more and more in harmony with those great purposes.

Gentle warning: I find it too easy to select and extract a verse or two which prove my point on some issue or other. I call this business of fine selection 'micro-reading'. It is as though I am looking at the holy text through a telescope held the wrong way around. Reversing the telescope, 'macro-reading', presents a wider and more comprehensively mature view of the wider purposes of God in creation which I otherwise would surely miss.

What he thinks will completely change how we think. What he says will completely change what we say. That possibility is so exciting.

Note
[1] Dietrich Bonhoeffer (1906-1945), *Temptation*, London: SCM Press, 1955

Chapter 17

INTERCESSION

After a significant length of practice in enjoyable prayer, I remain utterly convinced that we are here on this planet, first and foremost in God's' view, to be directly loved by him. That is the primary way in which he looks at us. Then, without any change of direction or strength of will, he wants us to be a centre for the onward distribution of his grace. We are the kingdom's ambassadors!

God is always looking at us from both these two similar angles: on the one hand as being people dedicated to himself and on the other hand we are here to play a part in his plan to reach other people.

I find that the 'Meeting Up' and 'Your Kingdom Come' phases of praying, as I have tried to describe them, both cement and grow my trust relationship with God a little bit every day, retuning and getting me in a right frame of mind to act as one of his prayer partners and kingdom ambassadors, and to do it using his dynamic outreach prayer tool – intercession.

For me, prayer always begins with the first two phases described in this book but reaches its zenith at the third. Essentially, 'Meeting Up' and 'Your Kingdom Come', phases 1 and 2, have only as much scope as I do, but phase 3, 'Prayers of Intercession', can take me anywhere around the world and frequently does just that. My experience encourages me to know that truly rounded prayer will always contain all three phases.

I would cheerfully suggest that the heart of any true prayer-giver has already caught a sense of warmth in God's heart and is prompted to reach out, arms outstretched, for the world. In fact the fundamental effect of Christian faith is that it changes our centre of gravity. Its effect on us is to move our hearts from being inside ourselves to being outside ourselves. It follows from this that being drawn upwards into coming face to face with his glory is a profound response to life – that is the 'Meeting up' with him phase and the 'Your Kingdom Come' phase that follows.

Intercession is how we reach out. It is the climax of three-phase partnership prayer, but it is only the fringe. Intercession's main direction is driving outwards.

To keep all this within its proper framework, I find it useful to remember from time to time throughout my day that there are a number of facts that underpin my prayer times – simple facts that I would share with anyone seeking the kingdom and seeking a deeper involvement in it. Everything depends on my coming at this from a right standpoint.

There are surely many ways of viewing this as there are many places from which to study any subject. From my own chosen viewpoint I have to be able to see it all with a wide-angle lens, taking in all the essential facts. If my vision of prayer does not do this, then the conclusions I come to may not be right ones, and I might easily be led off-piste in what I say and do as a result.

I cannot avoid these particular basic truths, either inferred or openly stated, that I keep finding in the Bible. They are woven into part of its history and its songs. From Genesis right through to the end of John the Divine's visions on Patmos, they underlie its prophetic writings from beginning to end.

Some of these have been so familiar to me over the years that I have fallen into the trap of taking them for granted. That being so, writing them down here is an excellent opportunity for me to refresh my memory with what is very old, as if newly discovered.

Firstly, the earth is the Lord's and the fullness thereof. It is his by dint of its creation and by his own sovereign rule.

Secondly, God gave his ruling authority over the earth to us – mankind.

Thirdly we – the human race as a whole, holding all this in trust from God – passed his rule over to somebody else. We were (and still are) deceived into doing this through a kind of double act. It is, at one and the same time, an act of disobedience and one of obedience. It is disobedient to God and at the same time obedient to someone else, a prince who wanted to get it all into his own hands.

This handover is portrayed in the Bible as having been done by the first people, Adam and Eve, but its effects continue to this day. As it goes on remorselessly, this continues to damage our relationship with God, shifting our allegiance away from him.

Thus, delegated authority in this Earth we have given away to someone else. It is increasingly under the control of that fearful prince whose name has changed to Satan, the hater, the enemy. If talk of Satan is distasteful then we might consider the way society moves relentlessly further into a world focused entirely on ourselves, what we want to think about, and what we want to do. Despite all this tragedy, God is still very eager to turn the world back to its original allegiance to him, and influence by him, for his own sake and for ours, for creation's sake. The world was originally designed to be a place where we would live for ever in a most friendly and peaceful relationship with God, a place with no sickness, no dying, no tears that might cause, or result from, anything that might come between us and the love of God. That world is still in the building.

It is not yet the world that God wants, though that will be some coming day. Sadly, life on Earth has been much scarred and changed for the worse under its present ruler. Most likely, Adam and Eve of the Bible's Creation story would not recognise their early home as they first came to live in it, fresh from the hand of its Creator.

The possibility of living a perfect life is on offer to everyone in the world. That offer is often thrown away by us. So a Man came from heaven, and while Jesus was perfectly and utterly human, he was a man quite distinct from everyone else. He is quite apart from every other person because he is more truly human than the rest of us. This Man was to head a movement intended to swing the world back on track.

Now these two, Jesus and the pretender-prince, had a running battle, the most terrific trial of strength ever waged or witnessed. It went on and on, from Herod's jealous fit of infanticide until the overwhelming grief of Calvary (and two days afterwards).

This spiritual battle went on throughout those thirty-three years with a ferocity never seen before or since. The subtle evil-prince Satan did everything he could through those early Nazareth years, then on into the wilderness, Gethsemane and as far as Calvary's crucifixion. At three o'clock that day the evil one imagined he had won. I suppose there must have been a great celebration party in the hot headquarters of hell. It would have appeared to them that the victory was theirs when Jesus lay dead in the grave.

The third morning came along and the bonds of death around Jesus were snapped as if they were rotten cotton. Jesus rose from the dead a conqueror. In that moment Satan knew he was defeated. He had lost everything. Jesus, divine and human, Son of God, had won.

Today we still have a few more troublesome facts to live with. Firstly, Satan refuses to acknowledge defeat. Secondly, he refuses to surrender his influence until he absolutely has to. He gives up only *what* he has to, and only *when* he has to. Thirdly, he is supported in his ambitions by the outlook of modern society. He has got society's consent to his control. The majority of people on planet Earth today have agreed to that control. We are becoming increasingly egocentric instead of God-centred, inward seeking instead of upward gazing. This central movement from God to self breeds a comfortable home for the enemy. Within this home he can run riot. He has this control only because of our consent – Satan cannot get into anyone's life without that agreement.

Well, where does that leave God's plan for the recovery of the world? He has left the war open, and the defeated chief remains on the field of battle. This seemingly strange and possibly unwelcome outcome is the way it is so that Jesus can win the whole race of humanity back to his Father's home again through our own change of heart.

The great and final pitched battle for our futures is yet to come. Jesus rides into the future fight already the winner. Satan will fight his last fight under the shadow of an unavoidable final defeat.

Now the phase 3 role of intercession prayer in all this ongoing strife is this: God is always seeking people, people who live in the world but are prepared to stand up as prayer partner, kingdom ambassadors against bad things in particular and evil in general – people who know at the bottom of their souls that Jesus is the winner. Satan knows it and is frightened of him. He must give ground before Christ's advance, and he must also surrender in front of this prayer partner ambassador who stands for Jesus – and surrender he most certainly will. Reluctantly, angrily, as slowly as he can get away with it, stubbornly contesting every inch of his retreat.

Thanks to the recognition of this divine prayer partnership, this 'sending out' example of Jesus to all, I must most heartily recommend that we all accept the offer of an ambassadorial role in the world – for the kingdom of God. If we do, how will it work?

Chapter 18

GET READY!

As it is in every other kind of partnership, at least two parties are involved. Both parties contribute to the arrangement, the subject of the partnership. Without both parties contributing, the whole begins to break down. In this working prayer partnership with God there are only two in the arrangement: the good Lord and the prayer-giver. God provides all the gifts necessary:

1. His Appointment
A role in implementing top kingdom-spreading policies is given over to us. He does not do all the major work himself, leaving us simply to tidy up any loose ends. He himself does all the difficult and stress-filled stuff, allowing us the joy of harvest. He has been described as the vine sending out roots into the deepest places of life while supporting all the branches. We are the branches and are allowed the joys and thrills of bearing the fruit.

'Very truly I tell you, whoever believes in me will do the works I have been doing, and they will do even greater things than these, because I am going to the Father.'
John 14:12, NIV

He has now given the lead responsibility for these greater works to us prayer-givers. I suppose that angels would have been thrilled to look after them but we mortals have been selected to take on this work.

2. Offering Training

God sees to it, individually, that all his own prayer partners are properly trained. Every effective employee and volunteer alike in any walk of life has to be trained up for the job to hand. In secular affairs, learning about the business or gaining a particular skill within it is a great advantage. In the prayer work of kingdom stretching, God himself prepares his prayer partners, on offering themselves for this service, for the work ahead.

> For we are God's handiwork, created in Christ Jesus to do good works, which God prepared in advance for us to do.
> *Ephesians 2:10*, NIV

3. Getting Us Ready

It's also God's practice to get us ready for this training and equipping, adapting to listen to his wishes and then to pray into his good works. The thought of being adapted like this should be quite acceptable to us, if only because some degree of change will always be necessary to make the natural human being suitably skilled for kingdom prayer work. Chickens on the ocean waves are quite lost at sea, sheep are in considerable danger trying to fly above the clouds and fish are quite lost when out of water! They are simply not adapted to doing these things. Every species, in the natural, has their own natural way of being what they are. Such natural ways will need adapting for kingdom prayer work.

Orange trees are grown for their fruit. Trumpets are made for making music and roses are designed and grown for their picturesque colour and gorgeous scent. We would be foolish to try to make a rose grow oranges, or to make a trumpet behave like a petrol engine. Our efforts would only be wasting time. In the same way, to expect an unchanged, unaltered although willing soul to do Christ's kingdom prayer work, through their joint prayer partnership, might only be wishful thinking.

For this reason, Christ, in moving things forwards, sharpens and sterilises his instruments. He gives his prayer partners a similar frame of mind, the reactions and the talents that cause us to pray towards his intended results, to love the ideas and principles of the kingdom and to accomplish them with him.

He specifically trains and moulds each one of us for the particular kingdom-stretching job assigned to us at the time. One of us may be called to pray for one particular aspect of the problem and another may be called to open a 'trapdoor', as it were, on a completely different aspect of the same difficulty. In the limitations of being human we may not even be able to make the connection between these two, but God knows his business. Then, being fitted together like the pieces of a jigsaw, we can, individually and privately, contribute our respective duties and responsibilities in prayer, unwittingly alongside all those others who might have been engaged on the same problem.

4. Resources

Sometimes, after prayer, our conscience might be moved to do some particular thing or say some particular thing to open doors for kingdom growth. This work, should it be needed, is paid for in advance. God supplies all the resources we will need for whatever our joint enterprise with him turns out to be. He does not send us out to work without sufficient materials, at least not when the direction of our efforts has been pre-determined in prayer. He invests all the resources we need in the partnership; himself. He does not even limit our expenses, but says to us,

> And God is able to bless you abundantly, so that in all things at all times, having all that you need, you will abound in every good work.
>
> *2 Corinthians 9:8*, NIV

5. Debts Disappear

God has taken our liabilities onto his own shoulders, written-off our past incidents of ungodly behaviour, even suffered the consequences himself of those bad choices. As well as all this, he has drawn us into fellowship with him and made us joint heirs of all heaven's riches of grace and glory.

6. The Spirit's Influence

Of course, we are very much the junior partner in this prayer relationship and in need of a lot of help from above. The all-seeing author of our personal spiritual programme and the source of all authority and power in this working prayer partnership is the Holy Spirit. God has promised him to us to help us:

> I pray that out of his glorious riches he may strengthen you with power through his Spirit in your inner being, so that Christ may dwell in your hearts through faith. And I pray that you, being rooted and established in love, may have power, together with all the Lord's holy people, to grasp how wide and long and high and deep is the love of Christ, and to know this love that surpasses knowledge—that you may be filled to the measure of all the fullness of God.
>
> *Ephesians 3:16-19*, NIV

We have to accept the truth that, without him and his gifts, we can do very little in this world that is acceptable to God or effectual in lasting and life-changing ways.

7. Teaching us the Scriptures

Through reading the scriptures and absorbing them we become thoroughly equipped for all his intended good, kingdom-stretching works. Working in a prayer partnership with God he will lead us on into the world of holy other-worldliness and like-mindedness with him in which we can be trained for kingdom work.

> Now may the God of peace, who through the blood of the eternal covenant brought back from the dead our Lord Jesus, that great Shepherd of the sheep, equip you with everything good for doing his will, and may he work in us what is pleasing to him, through Jesus Christ, to whom be glory for ever and ever. Amen.
>
> *Hebrews 13:20–22*, NIV

As we go along together in this prayer partnership, he shows us things which could only be spiritually discerned, at the same time preventing our words from being too loose and vain.

8. Getting things ready around us

God doesn't only get the instruments ready but the works as well. Again from St Paul:

> ..... good works, which God prepared in advance for us to do (*from Ephesians 2:10b*, NIV).

What a huge comfort this is to those of us who embrace the offer of a prayer partnership with him – that all the prayers and works we are called into are prepared for us in advance. This is important; we have only to step into them. These 'good works' of the kingdom are already being prepared for us. We followers are not supposed to dream up these works for ourselves but to receive them and wear them as if they were a new set of clothes.

We will have different parts to play, different roles to slip into the bottom of our hearts, especially as we develop into kingdom ambassadors (shown later). We might need the robe of wisdom, we might need to exercise power, at another time we may need extra compassion. Another time we might need to understand a particular person's way of thinking or weep with someone who is mourning. Again, we might need to warm up a cold heart; cheer up a depressed soul; lead a straying life back to our Saviour; to the divine healer.

All this is ready and waiting for us, laid up for us in Christ and only needing to be transferred across into our lives in the realities of joint action with our prayer partner. The object of this exercise is that it becomes not 'me' but Christ; not the follower's works but our Lord's works in and through the follower. We prayer-givers, operating in a prayer partnership with God, are the pen, not the hand that does the writing. We may indeed be the voice box but we are not the thought that says things by using it. We are only the water-bottle and the Lord is the priceless never-exhausted living water that fills it and pours out of it.

This all adds together to make our work really easy. Prayer partnership work is a spontaneous service; it is simply the overflow from any heart governed by the mind of Christ. Here Jesus describes true service in the Spirit, the sort of service we followers are involved in through our divine prayer partnerships:

'Whoever believes in me, as Scripture has said, rivers of living water will flow from within them' (*John 7:38*, NIV).

It is quite common enough for people to find that their day to day work is a drudge. True kingdom-stretching prayer partners of God soon find out that their Lord, their senior partner, carries both them and the burden. It is too easy for we religious folk to begin our work for God with great enthusiasm, doing our best to help him and his cause. We would do far better knowing that he does not really need us in our eagerness; it is then that we are happy and relieved to lay the burdens of his work back on him.

Working as an ambassador, a personal and private prayer partner with God to stretch his kingdom, is a little like a pencil listening to the pencil maker. The pencil maker takes the pencil aside, just before putting it into the box. 'There are five things you need to know,' he tells the pencil, 'before I send you out into the world. Always remember them and never forget and you will become the best pencil you can be.'

Firstly: you will be able to do many great things but only if you allow yourself to be held in someone's hand.

Secondly: you will have to experience a rather painful sharpening from time to time, but only if you are being worked with. You will need it to become a better pencil and to keep your effectiveness.

Thirdly: any mistakes you might make can be corrected.

Fourthly: The most important working part of you will always be what is inside and not what people might see of you.

Fifthly: On every surface we pencils are used on we must leave our mark. No matter what the conditions of that surface we must continue to write what we are directed to write.

God willingly takes both us and our prayer service into his hands. The best we can do about it is to rest on his breast and let him use us as he needs us. That is a vital part of the partnership.

... and to know this love that surpasses knowledge – that you may be filled to the measure of all the fullness of God.

Now to him who is able to do immeasurably more than all we ask or imagine, according to his power that is at work within us, to him be glory in the church and in Christ Jesus throughout all generations, for ever and ever! Amen.

Ephesians 3:19–21, NIV

9. Rewarding our efforts

What is the effort involved in being a prayer partner of God in the kingdom? Only this – to believe in the one that God has sent. We spend time in his company, listen for his planned guidance, pray straight the way ahead for him and watch for his results. God rewards his prayer partner's work and shares the reward with us as much as if we had done it all ourselves.

'When you enter a house, first say, "Peace to this house." If someone who promotes peace is there, your peace will rest on them; if not, it will return to you. Stay there, eating and drinking whatever they give you, for the worker deserves his wages.'

Luke 10:5–7a, NIV

We have no way of telling, in advance, what that reward might be but we do know something of the joy of bringing a soul to Jesus to find their faith in him or to find their healing. We know what it feels like to meet someone after a long time who tells us how something we said or prayed for might once have helped them. What will it feel like to meet up with them again in heaven, maybe bringing with them hundreds of souls they have gone on to help?

In this partnership, what do we bring to God?

1. Honour

A great deal of what we think of as everyday Christian work is just that – *our* work. God is often asked only to help it along with a blessing. When in prayer partnership with him, true kingdom work is given to him in response to him and carried out as being *his* work and at *his* beckoning. Kingdom-stretching prayer work is done under his absolute responsibility and ownership. He prepares it, initiates it and the prayer-giver then prays it and perhaps goes on to do it under his guidance. This partnership involvement can never be thought of as something we are doing for the Lord. It should always be a question of: What is the Lord doing *through* me?

Only in such divine prayer relationships might we hear far less about our church, our shared connections, our particular efforts, our work. Instead we would learn to go through life with the Lord for the sake of his kingdom work.

2. Knowing our need for partnership

We always need to remember that God could do all the things he prefers to use us to do, through his infinite power and ability and without us. Instead, he has appointed our involvement. God and the kingdom prayer partner who is made in his likeness can be walking and working side by side; the human prayer partner can enjoy friendship with him and be in service to him and to his kingdom.

God has already planned and arranged to supply the whole of creation with living water through the pipes and channels of his prayer partners' ambassadorial hands and hearts. It follows then that if we fail to fill our part in this partnership there will be a hiccup in the flow of supply.

With that in mind, I can only wonder at the grief I must sometimes be causing in heaven , with God knowing that the resources we need are enough for the whole of mankind and that their availability cost Christ's life-blood. I sometimes wonder if Christ is looking in vain for hands and hearts to carry out his grace-filled plans for this gone-astray world.

3. Working his way.

A lot of kingdom work manages to get disrupted and broken up because we want to do it our way rather than following God's leading. But if we really do intend to build in his temple then we will have to build according to his 'architect's drawings' and on the foundation he has put there for us, building with the materials he has supplied to hand for the work.

> They serve at a sanctuary that is a copy and shadow of what is in heaven. This is why Moses was warned when he was about to build the tabernacle: "See to it that you make everything according to the pattern shown you on the mountain" (*Hebrews 8:5*, NIV).

The church is not merely a place for group initiatives but a divine temple, built with divinely designed resources supplied by the Holy Spirit, using the labours of consecrated men and women. Where is the simplicity of the gospel? The apostles went out under the direction of the Holy Spirit. Natural gifts were not despised; everything was fused into the living fire of the Spirit, in power and holiness.

4. Working in his strength

We may be heavily engaged in some church activity or other which we believe is a good one, using our own human enthusiasm (or the enthusiasm of our leaders) to drive it. In such cases it is not always possible to draw on the strengths of God because we are perhaps too busy relying on ourselves for it.

We do, however, take his power into partnership for the spiritual work that he has ordained along our path and then, instead of the strain and toil of our own wisdom and skill, we can put on his strength and use a little of his infinite power. A touch of God's hand is worth a million human hands.

There may well be nothing new under the sun! This is the same old gospel. Let us allow it into the work we do in partnership with the Lord, as well as into our souls, and we shall find he is everything.

Chapter 19

GOD'S AMBASSADORS

When I did eventually join God's private Diplomatic Corps, what was my responsibility as a member of His Majesty's kingdom workforce? We are all, defines St Paul, ambassadors in Christ. We come from the kingdom of God/ heaven and live in a foreign country called 'the world'. It is there that we do our business, kingdom business.

Yet many of us may feel we are nowhere near clever enough or theological enough to be anyone's ambassador, let alone Almighty God and his kingdom; let alone having any authority over anything at all on his behalf, as an ambassador does.

Here is an encouraging thought from John Owen (1616-1683):[1]

When an unskillful servant gathers many herbs, flowers and seeds in a garden, you gather them out that are useful and cast the rest out of sight. Christ deals so with our performances. All the ingredients of self that are in them on any account He takes away and adds incense to what remains and presents it to God. This is the cause that the saints at the last day, when they meet their own duties and performances, they know them not, they are so changed from what they were when they went out of their hand. 'Lord, when saw we Thee naked or hungry?'

So God accepts a little, and Christ makes our little a great deal.

What a wonderful thought that is! Let us suppose that I did have ambitions to become an ambassador in some foreign country. There would be two essential things to organise right at the beginning of such a new direction.

The first and more important one of those would be to receive the appropriate official appointment. Nothing would even get started without this. Without an official appointment on paper I would need to keep very quiet to avoid raising too many eyebrows in the country I would be going to work in. To do this I would have to get into a particular and trusting relationship with the right government people, making sure I get from them the appointment as an ambassador and all the necessary official credentials.

Those official credentials would establish and authorise my ambassadorship to any overseas government. If I arrived in a difficult situation and held up those credentials I would immediately be recognised as representing the views and opinions of my home government. Those credentials would, too, give me the right to transact business overseas in our home country's name, on behalf of our country's interests. Indeed, my country's government would accept this and expect this from me.

Secondly, if I really was wise and clever enough to be an ambassador, as a matter of high priority, I would arrange to meet up with some predecessors in the job and have as many meetings with them as I could, learning all I possibly could from them about the country I was going off to serve in, principles to stick with and pitfalls to avoid.

The first of these tick boxes, the accreditation, would make me, technically, an ambassador. The second tick box would, I hope, give me some background skills as an Ambassador and make it appear that I know what I am talking about!

I needed to tick those same two boxes as I set off to learn and experience ambassadorial intercession. Firstly, the relationship between me and the home Governor (the Lord of heaven and earth) has to be established and set to grow before any inter-government business (kingdom business) can be transacted through my prayerful efforts. Then I need to set out to acquire some skill in transacting whatever business comes to hand.

The basis of an ambassador's praying is not found in learning the right words or in doing the right things. It comes quite naturally from our right relationship with God. It emanates from, and is taught by, the Holy Spirit, and heard more clearly through the constant practice of phase one.

In intercession prayer we recognise ourselves as being ambassadors, representing God's kingdom in this worldly world – representing our Lord's views and opinions in a foreign land – a land foreign to us – in the world.

Our need is to enjoy his willingness to be in a prayer partnership. It is a question of naturally knowing what he wants and insisting on his rights down in this earthly field of action. It means representing his views and opinions with delegated powers to back up those views, not merely derived from reading the right books or from working out the right theology but from practising working in a personal prayer partnership with him.

Clearly, the only basis for such a trusting relationship with God is Jesus. He came as both God and Man. He still reaches both with outstretched arms. He is the bridge. We get back to our heavenly Father through him. The sacrifice of the cross is the basis of all prayer. Through it the necessary relationship becomes established which underlies all prayer.

Out there in the world for the king and the kingdom of God/heaven we are never alone. Our lives are spent hand in hand with our divine prayer partner. By the operation of the Holy Spirit, we are taught how to think more and more as he does. We learn, through this partnership, built on in phases 1 and 2 identified in this book, to see the world as he sees it. We can speak accordingly to those people and ideas and forces that control it against his will. Jesus' own words have made this very clear to us. There is a positive assurance that whatever needs doing will be done. The reason for this is given:

'For where two or three are gathered together in my name, there am I in the midst of them.'

There is another way to put it: if there are two of us praying with each other, there are actually three. If three of us get together to pray, there will be four of us praying. There is always one more than we think there is. Where there is only me in my prayer time there are always two – me and my most holy prayer partner.

When the thought comes, from time to time, that I have such a simple brain that God could hardly stoop to do business hand in hand with me, I need to remember that the Father always hears Jesus. Wherever seriously searching and trusting hearts pray, Jesus is present, taking our prayer and making it his own prayer where it falls into the pattern of the Father's will and purposes.

There are no limits, in the Bible, to the things we ambassadors can ask for in this foreign land. There are, however, three limitations imposed on us. (1) Our prayer is to be through Jesus; (2) Kingdom of God/heaven's ambassadors are to be in the fullest harmony with his views and purposes; and (3) We must be expectant; we must trust. We must have righteous trust in God.

What, for the kingdom ambassador, is righteous trust? Ultimate confidence in the goodness of God's plan cannot rest solely on the intellectual or theological confidence in his goodness. If that is where it rests, such an optimism will surely suffer disillusion. Given time, romanticism will transform itself into cynicism as it always does, throughout history.

Kingdom ambassadorial trust is something quite different from common or garden optimism. It is trust in God, in a good God who created a good world, though the world is not now good; in a good God, powerful and good enough to finally destroy the evil that we do and get us all back again.

This kind of trust is not optimism. It does not rise up, in fact, until optimism breaks down and we stop trusting that we are always able, one way or the other, to solve the problem ourselves. Trust does not grow out of our intellectual understanding of God or even from witnessing some of his miracle working – it grows from a knowledge of our own inadequacies in the face of an evil world. Trust thickens and deepens as any kingdom of God/heaven ambassador operates confidently in the certain knowledge of his or her Government's attitudes, policies and strategies, and being assured of total support from that quarter. The ambassador of the kingdom of God/heaven, working in prayer partnership with Jesus to see his kingdom extended, lives and works with exactly that deep and reliable confidence.

The kingdom ambassador is absolutely key to the implementation of the great plan. You and I are the keys to the transformation of the world.

Note
[1] Included in An Exposition upon Psalm CXXX (1668) and in *Works of John Owen*, v. VI, New York: R. Carter and Bros., 1851.

Chapter 20

IMAGINATION – BENEFITS AND LIMITATIONS

Our third phase of prayer, Intercession, is real world-changing service. It is probably the spearhead form of service for any true prayer-giver who is trying to work with God's plan.

This is not really like any other type of service. It is superior to other kinds of work in one particular way – it has significantly fewer limitations. In every other way of serving other people, or in serving the church, we are always limited by time and space, by our own strength, our imaginations, money, equipment, material supplies and whatever difficulties come to the fore when we are involved in doing business with other people. The fact is that there is only so much we can do. It has certainly been my experience of being a prayer partner with God that prayer, gloriously, does not recognise any of these limitations. The beneficial results of Spirit-led intercessory prayer can bless people's hearts, minds and bodies, by-passing walls, unimpeded by locked doors, successfully avoiding any need for passports, fund raising, organising travel, visas and work permits – coming directly into vital touch with the person who is needing to be affected by God's grace.

We are all limited, in doing even the smallest works of service as they are generally understood, to working in the space where we happen to be at the time, within the distance our voices will carry, the length of time we can keep going before stopping to eat or catch up with some sleep. We can also feel quite limited sometimes by the seemingly impenetrable walls of other people's politics, prejudices and lack of enthusiasm.

It seems sometimes as though the variety of service priorities and understanding knows no boundaries. I can think of a number of these: the act of speaking about kingdom truths to a group, a congregation; to one person at a time; doing some badly needed kindness like supplying spare clothing or helping with a local food bank; teaching; giving money; giving medical aid; sending messages of encouragement; publishing endless amounts of literature. All this variety of outworking is, I am sure, in God's plan for extending his kingdom.

However, I remain convinced despite all these things, that the real victory in every God-supported service is won in secret beforehand, by prayer. This indispensable aspect of good service is the kingdom ambassador's attack on the enemy's works, securing the victory already won.

In this act of winning the battle beforehand, our imaginations are a great blessing to all of us, used correctly. We can imagine future experiences and improve on conversations of the past. We can see the characters and the action in paperback novels and imagine ourselves to be actually present in scenes portrayed in radio drama. Everyone has this splendid gift. If I were to be asked what I had for breakfast this morning I would immediately see an imaginary picture of the breakfast table and the plate laid out in front of me. That is memory; that is recalling an actual event.

Moving on from there, can I imagine a scene which is somewhere away from me? Can I imagine what it might be like to sit alongside a sick child or a church leader on the other side of the world, faced all about with a host of doubts and unbeliefs? Yes, I can. In doing so I also begin to imagine what I might say or do or pray in that situation. In doing so I am there in spirit, and through using my imagination I am in a manner of speaking projecting myself, my own personality, into that situation, as an ambassador of the kingdom of God.

In exactly the same way I can, in my spirit, present myself at a bedside, in a courtroom or in a family home. Using my imagination I can go anywhere in the world and pray.

This kind of ambassadorial prayer is an insistent claiming by a prayer-giver, often operating like this as an un-embodied ambassador roaming anywhere around the world where the King determines. The insistent claim is that the kingdom of God, the power of Jesus' victory on the cross over anything evil, could and should be extended to influence any situation.

Such prayer takes on the characteristic of the particular prayer ambassador. That prayer-giver has a spirit which becomes a strong and forceful thing. In praying like this, using our imaginations to allow it, we project our own personality into the spiritual realm which is affecting the trouble-spot. What a relief it is to know that God uses our own personalities! Whether we are shy and retiring or vibrant, noisy or quiet, outward going or inwardly depressed, God has chosen us to pray in a particular set of circumstances. We have discovered this pointer in our phase 1 listening and have picked up a subject to work with. Why? This is because God has chosen us to do it, using us and our personalities, as we are.

Being spiritual rather than a military or a physical force, our spirits have certain characteristics that are only to be expected of un-embodied spirits. An un-embodied spirit is not limited by space as we embodied folk are. It can travel as quickly as we can think. If I decide to go to Texas it will take three or four days (if not a while longer) to organise the trip and get from my office to where I need to be in that State.

On the other hand, my spirit can get itself over there

as quickly as I can think about it. I can think myself into Houston, Texas quicker than I can speak out the words and be sitting immediately by a friend's bedside in the famous cancer hospital in that fair city, or wherever else I need to be praying.

Although I live in the UK, I can instantly be in the chapel of a general hospital in Saskatchewan, Canada to encourage a prayer team who are meeting for the first time to pray kingdom healing into any receptive patients.

Happily, our imaginations are not kept in place by solid obstructions like the walls. When I came in to the office this morning I had to come in through the door behind me. I was obliged, by the very fact that my soul lives inside my physical body, to come in by that way.

Intercession prayer, using my imagination like this, is the business of projecting my spirit (my real and actual personality though not my body) into the place concerned. There I can do business alongside other like-minded spirits involved.

As an example, I've lately been praying every day for a very sick baby in a hospital incubator on the other side of the country. There are many others involved, too, in supporting the family through their prayers. It makes my praying for her very tangible. Every time I sit in my office and pray (by her bedside in my imagination), my prayer instantly covers the distance in between her and me, having an effect upon any troublesome spirits surrounding her.

As many other prayer-givers have done before me, I mapped out a daily schedule of prayer. Since then I have been learning increasingly to utilise this most constructive attitude of prayer, working as an ambassador with, and for, the Lord Jesus in the Holy Spirit's intent to advance the kingdom of God through the world.

This attitude of prayer has brought a refreshing simplicity

to my faith and a pleasant peace to my heart, every time I remember that, when prayers of this 'imagining' type are breathed out, my spiritual personality is being projected into where my heart needs to be. In effect, I am sitting at a bedside, around a conference table, by a graveside, in the private office of a leading politician or under a pulpit, anywhere in the world.

Once there, I can proclaim the power of Jesus' victory over the evil one in that place and on behalf of those faithful ones who are standing there for God. I need no special words, no special attitude. This is my own personality involved. I merely go where God needs me to go and state our case however I see fit in the moment.

That is being a kingdom ambassador. Should we not, every one of us, increase God's footprint down here on planet Earth? This is the battlefield of life in prayer.

Of course our human spirit never actually leaves the body during this life, leaving us behind to visit elsewhere. Intercession, in this context of our developing prayer partnership with our Lord, is a question of inviting the Holy Spirit to influence our own imaginative picture, emphasising aspects of the problem as a way of guiding us into his desired point of prayer.

God can go anywhere and do anything. I can only sit at my desk, body and soul, and submit my prayer share in the partnership. I need to open the trapdoors for grace that he determines and it seems most helpful, to my hearing him, to have him bend my imaginary picture of the problem, to lead me on.

Chapter 21

BEAUTY FROM THE ASHES

The time has come. The need and opportunity to build private and personal prayer partnerships with God has never been greater than it is today. Looking back over our history, the advent of the Reformation gave us Protestantism, and through it, we gave ourselves permission to think for ourselves. We began to think our own thoughts rather than accepting a position of deference to the church in all significant details of faith. This freedom was greatly encouraged (and is still so encouraged) through the Age of Enlightenment which taught us that our own thoughts are to be held superior to all others, even to God's.

Over those years, through Methodism, Pentecostalism, the Baptist movement and other streams, the age of denominationalism arrived and grew and now, despite the strongest efforts and hard work, is on the decline throughout Western Christianity. What will come next?

There is one genre of faith in the Western world where lights of hope are shining brighter. It is attendance at Cathedral Sung Evensong. Is that surprising? These occasions are growing with people attending who may not necessarily be committed to church membership but who recognise and revel in their own spirituality. The whole atmosphere, the architecture, its music, its other-worldliness, all contribute to an evening of off-planet life in touch with another reality in their own lives. We might constantly wonder if there are not millions more like this who are simply not in touch with Cathedral activities and thus unable to take advantage of them?

So many of us pray privately, outside the limitations of church services, concerning conditions of family, friends and, sometimes for the even greater catastrophes and their worldwide fallout. So many want God's help and ask for it with little hope of actually receiving it. The excitement of true prayer is that it puts the horse back before the cart, seeks first the kingdom of God and his righteousness and then enjoys the personal fulfilment that comes from being an appointed ambassador of that kingdom.

True prayer, in harmonic partnership, aligns the prayer-giver with God's purposes. On the other hand, random requesting prayers are words and heartaches thrown heavenwards in hope, but God does what he has already planned to do. The proper place for a true prayer-giver is to let the Kingdom in where God determines. In the Lord's Prayer it is *his* will that we are asking to be done, not our *own* will.

So it is that seeking unity of our minds with his righteousness (the mind of Christ) is something that is worked out on our knees, alone with God, with deepest reverence. We think of Jesus in the days of his earthly ministry praying to his Father, so should we not plan to meet God in private, regularly, with the door shut and the Bible open so that we can be fully trained and equipped for the holy partnership of prayer to which we are called?

When we do, then along will come the clearer vision of our personal positions in the divine plan, the greater purpose of our lives, a broader scope of worldly wisdom, real unselfishness, simple praying and expecting, the delights of fellowship that come from working with him. Then will come even more great victories for God in his world as our faith rises, fills the church vacuum, and becomes a greater influence on human affairs than the world has ever known.

We shall not begin to directly know about all these great victories until the moon and stars are gone and the dawn breaks on a newly created day when the dark ways and shadows that stain our world will be chased away by the brightness of Christ's presence, the glow of the glory of God. In the meantime, I remain utterly expectant that my own private prayer partnership with the Lord, by his grace alone, will bring its own reward: many crowns to take with me to heaven, to lay at his feet.

The man who will not act till he knows all will never act at all.
Jim Elliot (1927-1956), citing a popular saying of ancient Greece.

SOURCES AND RESOURCES

In working out my personal prayer life I have read, pondered and quoted from a wide range of other people's wisdom for which I am greatly blessed and more than grateful. These include:

Bonhoeffer, Dietrich (1906-1945), *Temptation*, (London: SCM Press, 1955)

Donne, John (1573-1631), *Works of John Donne*, vol. I, (London: John W. Parker, 1839)

Drayton, R. Dean, *Apocalyptic Good News: Christ in the Cosmos*, (Wipf and Stock, 2019)

Elliot, Jim (1927-1956), *The Journals of Jim Elliot*, ed. Elliot, Elisabeth (Revell, 1990)

Elliot, Jim (1927-1956), *Shadow of the Almighty: The Life and Testament of Jim Elliot*, Elliot, Elisabeth (Harper, 1958)

Fleming, Gordon S. D. *Quiet Talks on Prayer* (Revell, 1904)

Casey Jones, Revd Dr Winfield – various 21st Century magazine articles

Lawrence, Brother (c.1605-1691), *The Practice of the Presence of God* (1895)

MacDonald, George (1824-1905), *The Higher Faith* (1867)

Owen, John (1616-1683), A Discourse Concerning Holy Spirit [1674],

Owen, John (1616-1683), *An Exposition upon Psalm CXXX* [1668]

Ryle, J. C. (1816-1900), *A Call to Prayer* (American Tract Society, 1867)

Sayers, Dorothy Leigh (1893-1957), *Christian Letters to a Post-Christian World* 1969

ten Boom, Corri (1892-1983), Clippings from My Notebook: writings of and sayings collected, Nashville: T. Nelson, 1982

Williams, Roger (1603?-1683) *Experiments of Spiritual Life & Health* (1652)

THE FOUR PILLARS OF PRIVATE PRAYER

PILLAR: THE DIVINE VISION

God's dream is that Heaven and Earth should eventually become indistinguishable – the kingdom of God in reality; he desires that all mankind should live there; that we shall live this life in peace with ourselves, with each other and with God.

PILLAR: THE OTHER WAY

Mankind needs this kingdom to come during our lifetime, that God's will is done on Earth as it is in Heaven; turning instead towards a self-focused life is to turn away from God; God's arms are outstretched to heal the wounds of turning.

PILLAR: THE DIVINE PLAN

That the door between Heaven and Earth has been opened by the sacrificial crucifixion of God's Son, Jesus Christ; that the dividing curtain between Heaven and Earth is rent apart, allowing deeper access to the kingdom; that the restoring grace of God now flows unhindered into the world.

PILLAR: THE PLACE OF PRAYER IN THE PLAN

All righteous prayer emanates from God. Righteous and answerable prayer is God's communication with prayer-givers, instructing the opening of worldly 'trapdoors' to allow his grace to freely flow. Prayer-givers are required and equipped to be Ambassadors of the coming kingdom; to fulfil the Divine Plan we are called into the harmony of prayer partnership with the Holy Trinity as they are in harmony with each other. Thus it is that those who pray become the world's change-makers.

The wicked man flees though no one pursues but the righteous are as bold as a lion.

Proverbs 28:1

"We are so utterly ordinary, so commonplace, while we profess to know a power the twentieth century does not reckon with. But we are 'harmless' and therefore unharmed. We are spiritual pacifists, non-militants, conscientious objectors in this battle-to-the-death with principalities and powers in high places.

"Meekness must be had for contact with men, but brass, outspoken boldness is required to take part in the comradeship of the Cross. We are "sideliners"– coaching and criticising the real wrestlers while content to sit by and leave the enemies of God unchallenged. The world cannot hate us, we are too much like its own. Oh that God would make us dangerous!"

Jim Elliot (1927–1956), *Shadow of the Almighty: The Life and Testament of Jim Elliot*, Elisabeth Elliot (Harper, 1958)

Lightning Source UK Ltd.
Milton Keynes UK
UKHW020817100521
383461UK00016B/1161